# TEDDY BEAR
## *Centennial*
## — BOOK —

## BY LINDA MULLINS

Published by  Hobby House Press, Inc.
Grantsville, Maryland
www.hobbyhouse.com

# Dedication

*To all my wonderful friends and associates in the teddy bear world.*

## Other Teddy Bear Books by Linda Mullins:

Teddy Bears Past & Present, Volume I (Fifth Printing)
The Teddy Bear Men
Raikes Bear and Doll Story
Teddy Bears Past & Present, Volume II
Teddy Bear & Friends Price Guide
A Tribute to Teddy Bear Artists
American Teddy Bear Encyclopedia
Creating Heirloom Teddy Bears
A Tribute to Teddy Bear Artists – Series 2

Teddy's Bears
American Artist Teddy Bears – Patterns and Tips
A Tribute to Teddy Bear Artists – Series 3
Creating Heirloom Teddy Bears Pattern Book – Series 2
Handbook for Making Teddy Bears
Creating Miniature Teddy Bears
Linda Mullins' Teddy Bear & Friends Identification & Price Guide
Teddy Bear Centennial Book
Steiff Identification and Price Guide

All books published by Hobby House Press, Grantsville, Maryland.

Additional copies of this book may be purchased at $24.95 (plus postage and handling) from
**Hobby House Press, Inc.**
1 Corporate Drive, Grantsville, MD 21536
1-800-554-1447
**www.hobbyhouse.com**
or from your favorite bookstore or dealer.

Printed in the United States of America

ISBN: 0-87588-613-2

# Acknowledgements

A book of this type could not have been completed without the help and support of so many people. My heartfelt thanks in particular to my dear husband, Wally. With him beside me, all things are possible.

My deepest appreciation to my special friend Georgi Bohrod for her continued encouragement, assistance and professional guidance. Thanks also to Patricia J. Matthews for her computer service, to my patient and well-advising editor Sherry White, to Brenda Wiseman for her tireless creativity in designing this book, my photographer Bill Ahrend, and to my publisher Gary R. Ruddell for his continued faith in me that provides a means of sharing.

My heartfelt thanks to all the teddy bear artists whose magnificent bear creations grace the pages of the artist bear section. A great big thank you to my dear friend Ho Phi Le for his contribution of beautiful photographs of children with teddy bears and for the background and teddy bear photographs for the chapter openers. Special thanks to Rhys Berryman and Robert Michtom for their kind cooperation regarding pictures and information related to their grandfathers, Clifford Berryman and Morris Michtom.

My sincere appreciation to the following collectors for sharing pictures of their priceless collections with me: Dottie Ayers, Barbara Baldwin, Bill Boyd, Susan Brown Nicholson, David Douglas, Steve Estes, Margaret and Gerry Grey, Donna Harrison West, Barbara Lauver, Chuck and Cathy Steffes, Patricia Volpe, Susan Wiley.

My gratitude to the following companies for their assistance: Broadway Cares Fights Aids, Jean-Charles de Castelbajac, Cheju Teddy Bear Museum, Christie's, Comfort Cub Program, Dean's, Edinburgh Imports, Good Bears of the World, Gund, Hermann Teddy Original, Hospice, Huis ten Bosch, Japan Teddy Bear Association, Library of Congress, Merrythought Ltd., My Friends and Me, Muffin Enterprises Inc., National Portrait Gallery of London, North American Bear Co. Inc., Puppenhausmuseum, Reinhard Schulte, Yoshihiro Sekiguchi, Smithsonian Institution, Margarete Steiff GmbH., Steiff North America, Inc., Teddy Bear & Friends, Teddy Bear Museum, Teddy Bear Times, Teddy Bears of Witney, Teddy Today, The Bear Forest, The Toy Store, Toy Shoppe, U.S. Senate Collection for Legislative Archives, R. John Wright Dolls, Inc.

**Front cover cockwise from top left:** R. John Wright Dolls, Inc. *Clifford Berryman Bear®*. 2002.; American Bear. Circa 1907; Joan Woessner, Bear Elegance Exclusives, *Linda's Birthday Bear*; Ideal. *Smithsonian Bear*. 1903; Ideal Bear. Circa 1905; Steiff. *Henderson*. (Left) 1999, and Steiff. *Baby Alfonzo*. (Right) 1995; American Bear. Circa 1907; Steiff Bear. Circa 1904.

**Back cover clockwise from top left:** Beverly White, Happy Tymes. *Clifford Berryman Bear®*. 1996; Corla Cubillas, The Dancing Needle. *Two's Company*. 1996; R. John Wright Dolls, Inc. *Winnie-the-Pooh*. 1985; Ideal Bear. Circa 1905; ©North American Bear Company, Inc. *Muffy® VanderBear®* and *Hoppy VanderHare®*; "Yankee Doodle"; Helga Torfs surrounded by her bear creations. Collector's Bears by Helga Torfs; Janie Comito, Janie Bear. *Read Us A Story Grandpa Bear*. 1997.

# Contents

# *Introduction*

*Almost everyone has a special teddy bear in his or her life. Teddy bears are not merely a child's toy, nor just a highly valuable collectible item. In a century wrought with change and advanced technology, they represent a study in endurance of basic values. Teddy bears are as simple and individual as human emotions. The security of their touch, loyalty of their companionship, and the warmth of their adorable faces continue to bring out the best in human beings the world over.*

Since his introduction in 1902, the western world has embraced this cuddly, furry, lovable, durable and dependable friend and confidant. So popular is he that many individuals and companies claim to be his "parents." Today, teddy bears are still the predominant choice of soft toys for children all over the world.

The first catalyst in this latest surge of teddy bear collecting was Peter Bull's *The Teddy Bear Book* (1969). Bear collectors can be investors, aficionados or eclectic accumulators. But, they all search high and low for this symbol that exemplifies warmth and love. This love of bears has even created a new art form. The number of teddy bear artists, creating intriguing bears of all sorts and styles, is growing by leaps and bounds. These artists' bears may cost hundreds of dollars, and an early 1905 Steiff bear may double its market price in the next few years, but neither will ever be as emotionally valuable as any child's first bear.

Teddy bears have been popular for a long time, but their growing value as a collectible has only been accepted during the past twenty years. At the turn-of-the-century, children the world over fell in love with the soft, friendly stuffed animal. Now, men and women, young and old, novice collector and sophisticated dealer consider teddy bears from a different, more complex viewpoint. The study of bears became essential because of this modern development.

The more you know about bears, the more you'll enjoy their companionship. One look at a bear from years ago reinforces the evidence of the many levels and depth of their ongoing popularity.

This book came to be because I, too, love teddy bears and everything about them. As 2002 is the 100th anniversary of the creation of our beloved teddy bear, I felt a deep desire to author a book in celebration of this historical event. Therefore, within the pages of this book is a tribute to some of the wonderful people who have greatly contributed to the overwhelming success of the teddy bear in the collectible marketplace. I intend to share a personal outlook of teddy bears from their historical roots to their present day creations. I included some information about well-known handmade bear artists, stores, dealers, collectors and auctions. I will take you around the world to visit some of the most magnificent teddy museums. You will also learn about the magic of teddy bears and how these special toys can help people less fortunate than us.

So, please use this book as a guide and inspiration to enhance your understanding of these precious creatures. For more information and details, please refer to my earlier books listed at the front of this volume.

**OPPOSITE PAGE:** FACIAL APPEAL IS ONE OF THE MAIN POINTS TEDDY BEAR COLLECTORS LOOK FOR WHEN PURCHASING A BEAR. THIS LARGE REGAL-LOOKING 1905 STEIFF BRUIN IS ALSO EXTREMELY RARE DUE TO HIS SIZE OF 30IN (76CM) AND MAGNIFICENT PRESERVED CONDITION. *COURTESY BARBARA LAUVER.*

**LEFT:** SINCE THEIR INTRODUCTION INTO THE TOY WORLD IN 1903, THE GENTLE APPEALING FEATURES OF ALL SIZES OF EARLY STEIFF TEDDY BEARS CONTINUE TO BRING JOY AND LOVING SUPPORT. *COURTESY BARBARA LAUVER.*

**ABOVE:** EARLY 1900'S STEIFF TEDDY
BEARS WIN RECOGNITION AMONG
COLLECTORS BECAUSE OF THEIR APPEALING
CHARACTERISTICS AND EXCELLENT QUALITY.
THEY ARE AMONG THE MOST HIGHLY
SOUGHT AFTER COLLECTIBLE BEARS
COMMANDING THE HIGHEST PRICES TODAY.
*COURTESY STEVE ESTES. PHOTOGRAPHY BY
ALVIN GEE.*

**RIGHT:** THESE TWO EARLY 1900 AMERICAN
IDEAL MICHTOM-STYLE BEARS ARE VERY
RARE AND EXTREMELY DESIRABLE. NOTE
CHARACTERISTIC FEATURES OF THESE EARLY
IDEAL TEDDY BEARS—WIDE TRIANGULAR-
SHAPED HEAD, LARGE LOW EARS, LOW ARMS,
AND FOOTPADS COME TO A POINT. SIZES
12IN (31CM) AND 16IN (41CM). *COURTESY
BARBARA LAUVER.*

LEFT: IN 1907 WHEN TEDDY BEAR FEVER WAS RUNNING RAMPANT IN AMERICA, MANY OF THE COMPANIES MANUFACTURING TEDDY BEARS DID NOT USE ANY FORM OF IDENTIFICATION ON THEIR BEARS. THEREFORE, IT IS DIFFICULT TO POSITIVELY IDENTIFY TEDDY BEARS SUCH AS THESE ADORABLE EXAMPLES.

BELOW: THE GLOBAL INTEREST IN TEDDY BEARS BROUGHT ABOUT THE OPENING OF MAGNIFICENT MUSEUMS PACKED FULL OF WONDERFUL AND RARE TEDDY BEARS. VISITORS TO THE MUSEUMS CAN LEARN THE COMPLETE HISTORY OF OUR BELOVED TEDDY. THIS INTERESTING EXHIBIT AT THE *PUPPENHAUSMUSEUM* IN BASEL, SWITZERLAND DISPLAYS A REPRESENTATION OF AMERICA'S EARLY TEDDY BEAR SCENE. *COURTESY PUPPENHAUSMUSEUM, BASEL, SWITZERLAND.*

THE MAJORITY OF COLLECTORS LOOK FOR BEARS IN GOOD CONDITION AND SEE THEM AS A GOOD FINANCIAL INVESTMENT. THIS 16IN (41CM) STEIFF BEAR IN "WORN" SOLD AT CHRISTIE'S MAY 2000 AUCTION FOR APPROXIMATELY $2,440. IF THIS BEAR WERE IN "MINT" CONDITION, IT COULD COMMAND APPROXIMATELY $8,000 AND UP. *COURTESY CHRISTIE'S.*

RESEARCH HAS PROVEN THAT NO MATTER HOW TATTERED OR TORN AN ELDERLY PERSON'S BELOVED LIFE-LONG COMPANION BEAR IS, IT IS SOMETIMES THEIR LAST POSSESSION.

CERTAIN COLLECTORS OF ANTIQUE BEARS SEARCH FOR BEARS WHOSE LOSS OF FUR AND OVERALL WEAR PORTRAY YEARS OF LOVE AND CONSTANT ATTENTION. IN THIS CASE, FOR INSTANCE, THE WEAR TO THE RIGHT ARM DENOTES WHERE A CHILD HAS AFFECTIONATELY CARRIED HIS COMPANION.

Bears with provenance or documentation of their original owner are highly desirable among teddy bear collectors. This beautiful Steiff 1920 19-½in (50cm) bear was sold with a picture of the bear with its original owner (please refer to next illustration) at Christie's December 4, 2000 auction. *Courtesy Christie's.*

Photograph of bear in previous illustration (top left) with original owner. *Courtesy Christie's.*

Rare and mint condition early Steiff teddy bears can be found at Christie's South Kensington teddy bear auctions. Steiff Bear. Circa 1908. 16in (41cm); cinnamon mohair; shoe-button eyes; fully jointed; excelsior stuffing; printed Steiff button. Sold at Christie's May 25, 2000 auction for £7,050 (approximately $10,290). *Courtesy Christie's.*

LINDA AND WALLY MULLINS HAVE BEEN AVID TEDDY BEAR COLLECTORS SINCE 1976. A SPECIAL ROOM OF THEIR HOUSE IS DEDICATED TO SHOWCASE THEIR VAST COLLECTION.

CHRISTOPHER, SON OF TEDDY BEAR DEALER AND COLLECTOR BARBARA BALDWIN, SHARES THE SAME LOVE OF TEDDY BEARS AS HIS MOTHER. SHOWN HERE AT AGE 8, CHRISTOPHER IS HOLDING HIS FAVORITE TEDDY, A HUGE EARLY 1900'S STEIFF. *COURTESY BARBARA BALDWIN.*

PETER BULL IS CREDITED FOR HIS WORK IN BRINGING THE TEDDY BEAR COLLECTORS AROUND THE WORLD TOGETHER THROUGH HIS FIRST MONOGRAPH, *THE TEDDY BEAR BOOK* (1969, RANDOM HOUSE).

THE LOVE OF TEDDY BEARS HAS BEEN FURTHERED THROUGH ENGLISH LITERARY BEARS. OF COURSE, THE BEST KNOWN IS *WINNIE-THE-POOH*. HERE, A.A. MILNE, FAMOUS AUTHOR OF THE *WINNIE-THE-POOH* STORIES, SITS WITH HIS SON CHRISTOPHER ROBIN AND *TEDDY BEAR POOH*. MARY HILLIER, "A FAMOUS ENGLISH TOY FIRM." *TEDDY BEAR AND FRIENDS®*, WINTER 1985. *COURTESY NATIONAL PORTRAIT GALLERY OF LONDON.*

ACADEMY AWARD ACTRESS AND BEST SELLING AUTHOR PATTY DUKE (LEFT) TEAMED UP WITH PIONEERING TEDDY BEAR ARTIST ANN INMANN-LOOMS, OF ANNEMADE BEARS (RIGHT) TO PRODUCE A LINE OF ORIGINAL ARTIST BEARS. *FAITH, HOPE* AND *CHARITY* ARE THE PREMIER SIGNATURE EDITION INTRODUCED AT LINDA MULLINS' SAN DIEGO SHOW IN AUGUST OF 2001.

FRENCH DESIGNER JEAN-CHARLES DE CASTELBAJAC DESIGNED THIS MAGNIFICENT ACRYLIC AND POLYESTER WINTER COAT FESTOONED WITH 38 IDENTICAL BOUNCING BEARS IN 1990. *COURTESY JEAN-CHARLES DE CASTELBAJAC.*

*Chapter One*

# In The Beginning

*In this fast paced world, no other image represents human caring and love like the teddy bear. Now that we can go to the moon, cure rare diseases and run entire business enterprises without ever meeting in person, the teddy bear is a cuddly reminder of a nostalgic past.*

The bear has been revered and honored since time immemorial. In both the New World and the Old World, cultures celebrate the bear. Bears represent an immortal and vital part of initiation, symbolizing transformation, growth and renewal. Our view of the teddy bear is part of a natural evolution beginning with Native American tribes. Today, the teddy bear is our modern day talisman that makes us feel good. Its nurturing qualities have grown over the years since those early American times. Modern day collectors seem to acknowledge that deep sense within their souls and honor the bear for his lasting importance in our history and well-being.

# The Berryman Bear

The next historic depiction of the bear in American culture is clearly a direct link to the teddy bear. The political cartoonist, Clifford Berryman, created what was probably the most popular of all cartoon symbols, the little Berryman Bear. This bear came into being after news of President Theodore Roosevelt's refusal to shoot a defenseless captured bear during a Mississippi bear hunt (November 14, 1902). When the story reached Berryman at *The Washington Post*, the imaginative artist depicted this sportsmanlike incident on the front page (November 16, 1902). The public response was overwhelming. Berryman received floods of letters requesting repeats of the bear.

Even before that famous bear hunt, Roosevelt had been a familiar figure in Berryman's cartoons. Because of the association with Theodore Roosevelt, the popular little bear began to make regular "appearances" whenever Berryman drew the President. (When Berryman left *The Post* for *The Washington Star*, the bear went with him.)

ABOVE: ONE OF CLIFFORD BERRYMAN'S OWN MOST TREASURED POSSESSIONS WAS HIS COLLECTION OF AUTOGRAPHED PEN PORTRAITS OF FAMOUS MEN AND WOMEN. IT WAS ONLY APPROPRIATE THAT WHEN BERRYMAN RECEIVED THEODORE ROOSEVELT'S SIGNATURE, THE LITTLE TEDDY BEAR WITH WHOM HE HAD BECOME SO HISTORICALLY ASSOCIATED, SHOULD APPEAR ON THE PAGE ALSO. *COURTESY LIBRARY OF CONGRESS.*

TOP RIGHT: PEOPLE HAVE ALWAYS BEEN FASCINATED BY BEARS. AT TIMES, THEY HAVE WORSHIPPED THEM, OR HUNTED THEM, OR BOTH. CONVERSELY, AT OTHER MOMENTS, PEOPLE SEE BEARS AS CUTE AND CUDDLY. UNDOUBTEDLY, THE FACT THAT A BEAR STANDS UPRIGHT JUST LIKE A MAN ALWAYS LINKS US TOGETHER. *COURTESY MARY DOUDNA.*

RIGHT: A FAVORITE THEME FOR MANY AMERICAN TEDDY BEAR ARTISTS IS NATIVE AMERICAN BEAR WORSHIP. BEVERLY WHITE OF HAPPY TYMES COLLECTIBLES DESIGNED THIS UNIQUE PIECE ENTITLED, *TOTEM POLE BEARS.*

LEFT: ON NOVEMBER 16, 1902, CLIFFORD K. BERRYMAN DEPICTED PRESIDENT THEODORE ROOSEVELT'S REFUSAL TO SHOOT A CAPTURED BEAR DURING A 1902 MISSISSIPPI BEAR HUNT ON THE FRONT PAGE OF THE *WASHINGTON POST* AS PART OF A MONTAGE TITLED "THE PASSING SHOW". THE PUBLIC RESPONSE WAS OVERWHELMING. BERRYMAN RECEIVED FLOODS OF LETTERS REQUESTING "REPEATS" OF THE BEAR. *COURTESY SMITHSONIAN INSTITUTION.*

MIDDLE: BECAUSE OF CLIFFORD K. BERRYMAN'S ASSOCIATION WITH THE LITTLE CARTOON BEAR WITH TEDDY ROOSEVELT, THE POPULAR LITTLE CHARACTER BEGAN TO MAKE REGULAR APPEARANCES WHENEVER BERRYMAN DREW THE PRESIDENT. *COURTESY SUSAN BROWN NICHOLSON.*

BELOW: ON THE DAY OF THEODORE ROOSEVELT'S INAUGURATION, MARCH 4, 1905, BERRYMAN DREW TWO CARTOONS ON PAGE ONE OF *THE WASHINGTON POST:* "THE EVOLUTION OF THE ROOSEVELT BEAR" (BERRYMAN'S NAME FOR HIS CARTOON SYMBOL) AND "THE ORIGINAL ROOSEVELT MAN". THE ADORABLE ROOSEVELT BEAR CARTOON, BEGINNING WITH THE PRESIDENT'S CAPTURE OF THE BEAR IN 1902, DEPICTS STAGES OF HIS EVENTFUL LIFE UP UNTIL ROOSEVELT'S INAUGURATION DAY. *COURTESY LIBRARY OF CONGRESS.*

THE 1904 CLIFFORD K. BERRYMAN CARTOON "THIS IS
QUITE AS NEAR THE 'REAL THING' AS I WISH TO GET".
PEN AND INK DRAWING. BERRYMAN REPORTEDLY WAS
THE FIRST CARTOONIST TO PORTRAY PRESIDENT
THEODORE ROOSEVELT AS A TEDDY BEAR. *COURTESY
THE U.S. SENATE COLLECTION, CENTER FOR
LEGISLATIVE ARCHIVES. CLIFFORD BERRYMAN BEAR®—
J.S. INTERNATIONAL MANUFACTURING CO.*

A THREE-DIMENSIONAL PLUSH VERSION OF CLIFFORD K.
BERRYMAN'S FAMOUS *BERRYMAN BEAR* CARTOON
CHARACTER STANDS BESIDE A HAND-PAINTED PORTRAIT
OF HIS ORIGINAL CREATOR, CLIFFORD K. BERRYMAN.
*CLIFFORD BERRYMAN BEAR®.*

LEFT: RHYS BERRYMAN, GRANDSON OF FAMOUS POLITICAL CARTOONIST CLIFFORD BERRYMAN, PROUDLY DISPLAYS SOME OF HIS FAVORITE BERRYMAN CARTOONS.

BELOW: (LEFT AND RIGHT) RARE IDEAL GOOGLIE-EYED BEARS. 14IN (36CM); MOHAIR; EYES PAINTED GLANCING TO THE SIDE; OPEN FELT-LINED MOUTH; FULLY JOINTED; EXCELSIOR STUFFING. NOTE THE SIMILARITY OF THE EYES GLANCING TO THE SIDE AND THE OPEN MOUTH OF THE PLUSH BEARS TO CLIFFORD BERRYMAN'S BEAR DEPICTED IN THIS ORIGINAL BERRYMAN CARTOON (CENTER).

# Theodore Roosevelt

To back track a bit, it is always interesting to look at the man most often credited with being teddy's namesake...Theodore Roosevelt. He developed a great reputation as a hunter, but in fact, he dearly loved animals and nature. His passion for hunting bear in particular was not solely to kill them, but to observe their natural habits. The grizzlies became his favorites. After Berryman's famous cartoon, publicity connecting President Roosevelt with bears increased. "President Roosevelt had great success hunting bear at the White House Christmas morning. He started on the trail for the library, where the Christmas presents were assembled, and there he found three miniature bears waiting for him." (*New York Herald*, December 28, 1902).

The day after the article appeared, the President wrote Clifford Berryman a letter expressing his delight with the little bear cartoons that had followed the original of the notorious hunt. Although Roosevelt continued to call the little bruin a *Berryman Bear*, others gave him the moniker we have come to know him by...the teddy bear.

Soon novelty makers saw the opportunity to reproduce the bear as a toy. The "teddy bear" vogue swept the nation. Practically every major American city had at least one or two teddy bear factories. Never before had anything compared to the craze of the teddy bear.

LEFT: THEODORE ROOSEVELT BECAME SO IDENTIFIED WITH THE TEDDY BEAR, THAT THE REPUBLICANS ADOPTED THE POPULAR BEAR AS AN IMPORTANT AND MEMORABLE SYMBOL FOR THE PRESIDENT'S ELECTION CAMPAIGNS. (RIGHT) TEDDY ROOSEVELT (TEDDY BEAR) CAMPAIGN PIN 1904. 3IN (8CM).

RIGHT: TEDDY AND THE BEAR IRON MECHANICAL BANK BY J AND E STEVENS COMPANY. 1907. AMERICAN BEAR. CIRCA 1907. 12IN (31CM).

So associated did Roosevelt become with the teddy bear, the Republicans adopted the popular bear as an important and delightful symbol for the President's election campaigns. Political postcards, trays, pins and mementos of all descriptions depicted Roosevelt with his friendly little companion.

Roosevelt's declaration that he would not be a presidential candidate in 1908 sent ripples of concern through the toy industry that the teddy bear craze was over. However, the teddy bear had already powerfully impacted the toy industry and American culture and continued to thrive.

Teddy Roosevelt's great accomplishments as a man and United States President will always be remembered, but the special toy to which he lent his name way back years ago will be with us forever. We honor Roosevelt for his part in the evolution of our undaunted little friend, the teddy bear, a toy that will continue to spread love, happiness and friendship throughout the country and the world.

The depth of the Roosevelt and Berryman affiliation and their individual stories so fascinated me that I made a special pilgrimage to Washington D.C. and The Library of Congress. The result was an entire book on the subject of Clifford Berryman and Theodore Roosevelt entitled *The Teddy Bear Men*. If you want more details on the important role this saga plays in the development of the American teddy bear, please refer to that book!

## Who Deserves the Credit?

There is much controversy surrounding the birth of the teddy bear. Everybody likes to take credit for inventing this special creature. It is not surprising that four people are credited in their obituaries with creating the Teddy Bear: Clifford Berryman, Margarete Steiff, Morris Michtom and Seymour Eaton. For instance, the Ideal Toy Company (see page 28) certainly claims to be one of the first to jump on the bandwagon in America.

Across the ocean, the Steiff Company states that it was creating its own version of a furry bruin in 1902. In Patricia N. Schoonmaker's book, *A Collector's History of the Teddy Bear*, articles taken from October and November 1906 issues of *Playthings* states, "Teddy Roosevelt's increasing popularity and the continuation of Clifford Berryman's cartoon featuring the appealing little bear were the best promotion the Steiff bears could have." So internationally associated was Teddy Roosevelt with the teddy bear toy, in 1908, Steiff re-named *Barle* (name for Steiff's toy bear creation) to *Teddy Bear*!

ROOSEVELT MEMORABILIA MAKES AN INTERESTING SCENE. (LEFT TO RIGHT) COLUMBIA TEDDY BEAR MFRS. *ROOSEVELT BEAR.* CIRCA 1907. 18IN (46CM). WHEN TUMMY IS PRESSED, MOUTH OPENS SHOWING TEETH MIMICKING ROOSEVELT'S FAMOUS SMILE. 1905 TEDDY ROOSEVELT POSTCARD, TR BOOK, IDEAL GOOGLIE-EYED BEAR. EARLY 1900'S. 9IN (23CM). (BACKGROUND) TEDDY ROOSEVELT BULL MOOSE SCARF. CIRCA 1912. TEDDY ROOSEVELT TAPESTRY. EARLY 1900'S.

## The Roosevelt Bears of Seymour Eaton

Clifford Berryman never referred to his famous creation as a teddy bear. He called it a Roosevelt Bear. Others called it a Berryman Bear. A notable series of bear-related children's books were written in the early 1900's with the same family name as the President. *The Roosevelt Bears*, created by Seymour Eaton, were two huge bears named *Teddy B* and *Teddy G* (B for black and G for gray, not bad and good as some people think.) The Roosevelt Bears look more like real bears than Teddies, but their influence on the toy bear market was tremendous.

Due to lack of identification or documented history, many American bears are unidentifiable. However, due to extensive research of old *Playthings* magazine ads, identifying these three wonderful early-American bears is possible. (Left to right) Aetna. 1907. 16in (41cm); mohair; glass eyes; card-board-lined foot pads. Bruin Manufacturing Co. (B.M.C.) Circa 1907. 13in (33cm); mohair; shoe-button eyes; woven silk label on foot reads: "B.M.C.". National French and Novelty Company. 1924. 14in (36cm); mohair; sleeping celluloid eyes.

By 1907, most every major city in the United States had a teddy bear factory. Like many American bears, due to lack of identification, the manufacturer of these two splendid, mint condition domestic bears is unknown. Note the short mohair, long narrow torso, large head and short snout on these bears—all characteristics of early American bears. *Courtesy Barbara Lauver.*

*Chapter Two*

*T*ribute
to *T*eddy *B*ear
*M*anufacturers

*Companies manufacturing
Teddy Bears possess unique
histories. The following
information offers understanding
of some of the best and pioneers
in the field. Please see my
earlier books for complete details.*

# American Teddy Bear Manufacturers

For a detailed catalogue of American Bear Manufacturers, please refer to my book, *American Teddy Bear Encyclopedia.*

## Ideal Toy Company

Ideal began as a mom and pop operation sewing teddy bears in their store. Over the years it grew to a large conglomerate. Even though there has been much controversy about the role of the Ideal Toy Company in the birth of the teddy bear, there is no doubt that the New York Stock Exchange-listed firm is greatly responsible for the popularity of teddy bears both in this country and abroad.

Legend has it that in 1902, when Morris Michtom (Ideal's founder) saw the now-famous Clifford Berryman cartoon of President Roosevelt's encounter with a bear, he was inspired. His wife Rose, stitched a lovable, jointed bear by hand and the couple displayed their creation in the window of their small store in Brooklyn, New York. They say that Michtom then wrote to Teddy Roosevelt to elicit his permission to name the animal *Teddy's Bear.*

When Butler Brothers, a large wholesaler who knew a sure thing when they saw one, bought all of the bears the Michtoms had already made, the idea took off like wildfire. The Ideal Novelty Company was born. The firm really solidified in 1907 after it moved to Brooklyn and produced is first American character doll. At that point, Ideal used the words that they were "the largest bear manufacturers in the country." In 1912, Michtom changed his company's name to Ideal Novelty and Toy Co.

That same year, Abraham Katz, Michtom's nephew, joined the company. He grew to play a major role in its success staying with the firm for more than 60 years. Morris Michtom's son, Benjamin, entered into his father's business in 1923 and grew to be a highly respected marketer with the toy industry.

In 1938, the company name was shortened to The Ideal Toy Company. In 1983, CBS bought Ideal for $58 million. View-Master (makers of the 3-D viewers) purchased Ideal, and in 1989, the toy company was made part of Tyco Toys, Inc. Ideal became an indirect wholly owned subsidiary of Tyco Toys. In 1998, Mattel bought the Ideal name.

When Morris Michtom died in 1938, his beloved toy business continued in the trusting hands of his family. Ideal never compromised the fun and quality toys it produced for several generations of America's children.

---

### Teddy Bear

Morris Michtom, Russian Jew who was president of the Ideal Novelty and Toy Company of New York, died Thursday morning after a long illness at the age of 68. It might seem from the name of the enterprise which he headed that it was just another commercial venture, making its uncertain way among those which follow the path of childhood fancy. But he invented the Teddy Bear, from which derived the many stuffed and hence soft and comforting dolls which little children cuddle frankly with wide eyes while awake in a perplexing world, or clasp to the throttling point while asleep.

It is a charming paradox that the animal which in life is so much feared, though wrongly as far as most species are concerned, should become the loved and frayed companion of the very young. Yet the Teddy Bear's guileless, shoe-button-eyed countenance, soft fur and yielding inner substance explain it all. They explain also the instinct for a defence against the hazards of the day and of the dark. The finest defence, greater than guns or adult words, is a companion who is always in agreement and always has the comforting word upon the tip of his tongue, even though he does not speak. It is very strange that it takes grown men and women so long to learn this anew, after the hiatus of their adolescence. Indeed we think the adult world would be much better with more of the Teddy Bear influence in it.

LEFT: ONE OF THE MANY ARTICLES WRITTEN IN THE DAYS FOLLOWING MORRIS MICHTOM'S DEATH. THIS ONE IS FROM THE PROVIDENCE JOURNAL JULY 28, 1938.

OPPOSITE PAGE: IN 1963, BENJAMIN MICHTOM PRESENTED THIS EARLY 1900'S IDEAL TEDDY BEAR TO PRESIDENT THEODORE ROOSEVELT'S GRANDSON, KERMIT, AND HIS FAMILY. THE ROOSEVELTS DONATED THE TEDDY BEAR, NAMED FOR THE PRESIDENT, TO THE SMITHSONIAN INSTITUTION IN JANUARY 1964. *COURTESY SMITHSONIAN INSTITUTION.*

VERY RARE IDEAL "GOOGLIE-EYE" BEARS. EARLY 1900'S. 20IN (51CM) AND 6IN (15CM). NOTE THE SIMILARITY OF THE EYES GLANCING TO THE SIDE TO CLIFFORD BERRYMAN'S FAMOUS LITTLE CARTOON BEAR (PAGE 19).

BENJAMIN MICHTOM, SON OF MORRIS MICHTOM THE FOUNDER OF THE IDEAL NOVELTY TOY COMPANY, STANDS IN FRONT OF A CASE, DISPLAYING ONE OF THE EARLY IDEAL TEDDY BEARS IN THE LEFT-HAND CORNER. NOTE THE RESEMBLANCE TO THE DESIGN OF THE EARLY IDEAL BEARS IN THE ILLUSTRATIONS ON PAGE 31. PICTURE FROM COLLIER'S MAGAZINE, DECEMBER 17, 1949.

ROBERT MICHTOM, GRANDSON OF MORRIS MICHTOM THE FOUNDER OF THE IDEAL TOY COMPANY, PROUDLY SHOWS A PICTURE OF HIS GRANDFATHER AND ONE OF THE EARLY 1900'S IDEAL MICHTOM-STYLE BEARS.

IDEAL BEAR. CIRCA 1905. 13IN (33CM); GOLD MOHAIR; SHOE-BUTTON EYES; FULLY JOINTED; EXCELSIOR STUFFING. NOTE FEATURES CHARACTERISTIC OF EARLY MICHTOM-STYLE IDEAL BEARS: WIDE TRIANGULAR-SHAPED HEAD, LARGE LOW EARS, NOSE EMBROIDERED WITH BLACK PEARL COTTON, LOW ARMS, AND FOOT PADS COME TO A POINT. A LARGE PERCENTAGE OF THESE IDEAL BEARS HAVE FIVE FLOSS CLAWS. SCHOENHUT THEODORE ROOSEVELT DOLL. 1909. 8-½IN (22CM).

IDEAL BEAR. CIRCA 1908. 16IN (41CM); BEIGE MOHAIR; SHOE-BUTTON EYES; FULLY JOINTED; EXCELSIOR STUFFING. COLLECTION OF RARE TEDDY ROOSEVELT CAMPAIGN PINS COVER BEAR'S COAT.

YOUNG AND OLD ALIKE NATIONALLY RECOGNIZE OUR ALL-AMERICAN HERO, *SMOKEY BEAR*. *SMOKEY BEAR* IS SYNONYMOUS WITH FOREST FIRE PREVENTION. THE "GUARDIAN OF THE FOREST" IS PHENOMENALLY POPULAR. HIS ACHIEVEMENTS AS "SPOKESBEAR" FOR THE COOPERATIVE FOREST FIRE PREVENTION ADVERTISING CAMPAIGN ARE UNBEATABLE. IN 1953, THE IDEAL TOY COMPANY CREATED ONE OF THE FIRST LICENSED *SMOKEY BEAR* TOYS OFFERED ON THE MARKET. HE HAD A MOLDED VINYL HEAD, HANDS AND FEET AND A PLUSH BODY.

# Gund Inc.

Gund was founded by German immigrant Adolf Gund in Norwalk, Connecticut in 1898. Company records show that when a toy buyer asked Adolph to make a teddy bear, he purchased a few yards of plush, took everything he needed home with him, and sat up nearly all night to make four sizes of teddy bears from 10in (25cm) to 16in (41cm). That was the turning point for his company.

In 1907, Gund moved the business to New York, and in 1910, he officially incorporated the company and introduced its first full line of stuffed toys. When Adolf Gund sold the business to his protégé, Jacob Swedlin, the firm continued to prosper with a line of velveteen animals that did acrobatics in 1927.

Throughout the 1960's, Gund continued to be best known for its Disney plush toys. Its *Winnie-the-Pooh* exclusives for Sears and its Collector Classics line were extremely popular in the 1970's, and its *Luv Me Bear* was its best seller.

The famous "Gotta Getta Gund" advertising campaign was launched in 1979. Today, Gund, which is based in Edison, New Jersey, maintains a showroom in New York City and employs about 200 people.

GUND *BEAR ON WHEELS*. 1927.
*COURTESY GUND*.

GUND. *TEDDI GUND*. CIRCA 1940. 16IN (41CM); GOLD MOHAIR;
INSET SNOUT; GLASS EYES; F.J.; K.S. NOTE: LARGE HEAD; LARGE
SLIGHTLY CUPPED EARS; SHIELD SHAPED NOSE; STITCHED MOUTH
FORMS SMILE; THIN FELT PAW PADS; EXTERIOR STITCHING (VISIBLE).
MANUFACTURERS LABEL WAS STITCHED INTO SEAM OF BODY OR
ARM—ALL CHARACTERISTICS OF *TEDDI GUND*. COURTESY GUND.

SCHLEPP IS AN AWARD WINNING GUND BEAR WITH A LOVER'S PHILOSOPHY, "THE BIGGER THE HUG, THE BETTER." HE HAS A GREAT PERSONALITY AND A THOUGHT-PROVOKING FACIAL EXPRESSION. TEXTURED PLUSH WITH A SOFTLY BEAN STUFFED BODY MAKES THIS GUY DEFINITELY ONE OF THE MOST HUGGABLE BEARS AROUND. PRODUCED IN BROWN AND WHITE IN SIZES 18IN (46CM) AND 14IN (36CM). COURTESY GUND.

SNUFFLES® HAS BECOME A GUND ICON TOO AS ONE OF THEIR BEST-SELLING STYLES. INTRODUCED IN 1980, HE NOW COMES IN VARIOUS SIZES AND COLORS. WHEN IT COMES TO HUGGING, HE'S NO AMATEUR. THAT'S WHY IT'S NO SURPRISE THAT SNUFFLES HAS LONG BEEN ONE OF GUND'S MOST POPULAR BEARS. COURTESY GUND.

# North American Bear Co., Inc.®

In the mid 1970's, while raising a small child and studying ceramic toy design, Barbara Isenberg decided to start a toy company which would produce uniquely designed, high quality teddy bears. The bears would have the nostalgic charm of antique toys with an appeal for both children and adults. She asked her fashion designer friend, Odl Bauer, to make a bear out of an old sweatshirt that would be soft, cuddly and different from anything else on the market. That bear evolved into *Albert the Running Bear*, a classic bear in a colorful running suit.

A year after *Albert the Running Bear* was produced, the Very Important Bears (V.I.Bs®) were introduced. The V.I.Bs took the world by storm with their velour bodies in striking colors, elaborate outfits and appealing pun names like *Humphrey Beargart*, *Bearilyn Monroe*, *Albeart Einstein*, *Bearb Ruth* to name a few. V.I.Bs continued as an important part of the collectible bear market until their retirement in Fall 1999.

Soon after the V.I.Bs appeared, NABCO introduced the classic, fully-jointed *VanderBear Family*® in 1983 and *Muffy VanderBear*® in 1984. Loyal *Muffy*® fans, enamored with her diminutive 7in (18cm) size, wonderful wardrobe and fun adventures, transformed her into a collectible and encouraged the formation of NABCO's international Muffy VanderBear Club in 1990 and Muffy Kid's Club in 1999.

Today, Founder/Creative Director Barbara Isenberg heads the New York Studio where all of the products are created by an in-house team of designers and artists. Finance, sales, and the warehouses are located in Chicago and headed by Chief Executive Officer Paul Levy.

OPENING CELEBRATION OF THE PREMIER MUFFY BOUTIQUE IN THE FLAGSHIP NEW YORK CITY FAO SCHWARZ TOY DEPARTMENT STORE ON OCTOBER 2, 1999. (LEFT TO RIGHT) KATYA BAUER, DESIGN TEAM MEMBER. *HOPPY VANDERHARE®, MUFFY VANDERBEAR®*. BARBARA ISENBERG, FOUNDER AND CREATIVE DIRECTOR. © NORTH AMERICAN BEAR CO.

OPPOSITE PAGE: *CANDY HEARTS*, NEW FOR SPRING 2001. *MUFFY VANDERBEAR®* SENDS "SWEET TALK" AND "BEAR HUGS" TO ALL HER "SWEET HEARTS" VIA *LULU MACFLUFF™* WHO DELIVERS THE CANDY GRAMS WITH "PUPPY LOVE". © *NORTH AMERICAN BEAR CO.*

LEFT: *RUGGLES™*. ONE OF NABCO'S MOST POPULAR, AWARD WINNING CLASSIC BEARS, *RUGGLES™* IS IRRESISTIBLE WITH HIS SCRUFFY HONEY-BROWN FUR AND WHIMSICAL APPEARANCE. © *NORTH AMERICAN BEAR CO.*

BELOW: *VANDERBEAR FAMILY® GARDEN PARTY*. STROLLING THROUGH THE BEAUTIFUL GARDENS, THE *VANDERBEARS* ENJOY THE EARLY FLORAL SCENTS IN SPRINGTIME FINERY. © *NORTH AMERICAN BEAR CO.*

# R. John Wright —
# R. John Wright Dolls, Inc.

R. John Wright has won a large following in the world of collectible bears and animals. All work is performed at the company workshop located in upstate New York by skilled artisans under the direct supervision of John and his wife, Susan.

The company is renowned for the highest quality design and craftsmanship and has a strong tradition of characters based on classic children's literature. In addition to the award-winning work with *Winnie-the-Pooh*, these include animals from the famous Beatrix Potter™ books, the mischievous monkey, *Curious George*®; Britain's other literary bruin, *Paddington Bear*™; and most recently the *Clifford Berryman Bear*® made to commemorate the 100th birthday of the teddy bear.

LEFT: R. JOHN WRIGHT, R. JOHN WRIGHT DOLLS, INC.

RIGHT: BASED ON THE FAMOUS CHARACTER IN THE *PADDINGTON* BOOKS BY MICHAEL BOND. ALPACA, FULLY JOINTED, MOLDED LEATHER NOSE, GLASS EYES, FELT DUFFEL COAT AND HAT AND CUSTOM LEATHER SUITCASE. LIMITED EDITION 2500.

FAR RIGHT: R. JOHN WRIGHT, R. JOHN WRIGHT DOLLS, INC. *NIGHTTIME WINNIE-THE-POOH*. 1998-1999. 12IN (31CM); LIMITED EDITION OF 2500.

Paddington Bear TM ©Paddington & Co. Ltd. 2000 Licensed by ©opyrights/

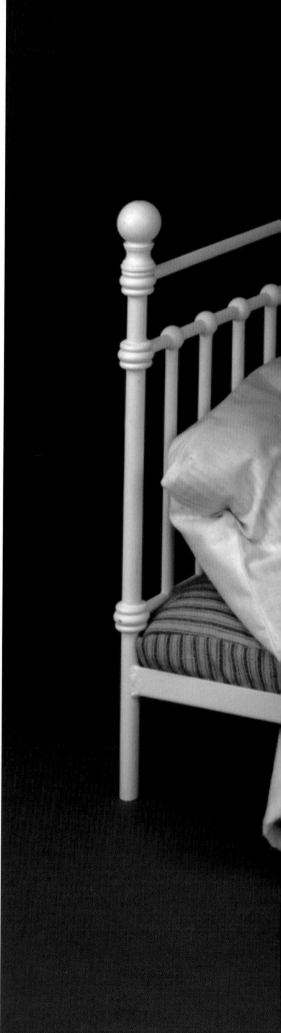

©Disney. Based on the "Winnie-the-Pooh" works. © A. A. Milne and E. H. Shepard.

**RIGHT:** RIGHT: R. JOHN WRIGHT DOLLS, INC. *CLIFFORD BERRYMAN BEAR®*, 2002. 13IN (33CM); HIGH QUALITY ALPACA PLUSH; LEATHER COVERED GOOGLIE EYES; MOLDED LEATHER NOSE; FULLY JOINTED. LIMITED EDITION OF 1000. A SPECTACULAR RENDITION OF CLIFFORD K. BERRYMAN'S FAMOUS CARTOON BEAR CUB.

**BELOW:** R. JOHN WRIGHT DOLLS, INC. *THE BABY BEAR COLLECTION*, 2000. THIS SERIES CONSISTS OF FIVE CUBS. (LEFT TO RIGHT) PANDA, BROWN, POLAR, BLACK AND KOALA (NOT SHOWN). EXTENSIVELY RESEARCHED, EACH 12IN (31CM) CUB IS MADE OF THE FINEST MOHAIR PLUSH, FULLY JOINTED, AND FEATURES TRUE-TO-LIFE DETAILS SUCH AS FELT PAW PADS, RESIN CLAWS AND GLASS EYES. IN ADDITION, EACH BABY HOLDS AN EDIBLE INDIGENOUS TO ITS HABITAT. MADE IN AN EDITION OF 500 EACH.

# German Teddy Bear Manufacturers

Germany was already renowned through Europe and America for its fine craftsmanship in early toys during the late 17th century. Many companies were family owned beginning their businesses from their home and growing into recognized leading manufacturers by the early 1900's. The oldest and most well known of these firms in the teddy bear world is Steiff.

## Steiff

If Teddy Roosevelt was the father of the Teddy Bear, Margarete Steiff is certainly the mother. Stricken by polio as a child, the young girl lived happily in a picturesque German village of Giengen-on-the-Brenz. In 1880, she showed her imagination as a seamstress. She conceived the idea of sewing an elephant into the form of a pincushion. Soon, Margarete created a menagerie of felt animals including pigs, monkeys, donkeys and camels. Her brother Fritz marketed the soft animals at local fairs.

By the turn-of-the-century, Margarete's nephews (Paul, Richard, Hugo, Otto and Ernest) joined her and turned the soft felt toys into a big business. Margarete's nephew, Richard, who joined the company in 1897, conceived the idea to design a young bear, which had movable joints like a doll. Richard maintained that such a character could be dressed and cuddled and loved and he was right.

Richard took the new movable bear to the Leipzig Trade Fair in 1903. Little attention was paid to the modest toy displayed at the Steiff exhibit. But as fate would have it, an American buyer (from the George Borgfeldt Co.) saw the model bear and ordered 3,000 to be made. Quickly the order was increased to 6,000 and by the end of the year, Steiff had sold 12,000 of the soft, all-jointed fur bears. The Steiff Company calls 1907 the Year of the Bear (in German, *Bärenjahre)*. Steiff bears reached a record sale of nearly 1,000,000 units in that year.

Early 1900 Steiff bears are undoubtedly one of the most collectible bears today. Their beautiful and distinguished characteristics, high quality of craftsmanship and unique features not only make them very desirable, but extremely difficult to locate. The elongated nose, arms, feet and hump give them a style that when studied is easier to recognize than most other bears. The definite, identifiable trademark introduced in 1905, was the small metal button marked with the Steiff name that is affixed to the left ear. Steiff brings nearly 200 new items onto the market each year. Today its collection features at least 850 articles.

Margarete Steiff died in 1909, but her love lives on in her toys. I think she would feel happy and proud to know that her family still religiously maintains her motto, "Only the best is good enough for our children" over 100 years later.

MARGARETE STEIFF'S MOTTO, "ONLY THE BEST IS GOOD ENOUGH FOR OUR CHILDREN" IS STILL RELIGIOUSLY MAINTAINED OVER 100 YEARS LATER BY HER FAMILY. *COURTESY STEIFF.*

RIGHT: IN 1904, STEIFF JOINTED THEIR BEARS WITH "METAL RODS" CONNECTING JOINTS. THIS EARLY METHOD OF JOINTING WAS DONE ONLY FOR A VERY SHORT TIME. THESE BEARS (28PB) CAME WITH AN ELEPHANT BUTTON AND A SEALING WAX NOSE. THEIR BODIES ARE FIRMLY STUFFED WITH EXCELSIOR, AND THEY HAVE FIVE EMBROIDERED CLAW STITCHES. THEY CAME IN SIZES 16IN (41CM) AND 20IN (51CM). *COURTESY DOTTIE AYERS.*

BELOW: STEIFF BEARS. CIRCA 1905–1907. 28IN–30IN (71CM–76CM). WHITE AND CINNAMON-COLORED MOHAIR STEIFF BEARS ARE AMONG THE RAREST AND MOST DESIRABLE. NOTE THE BEAUTIFUL ELONGATED FEATURES CHARACTERISTIC OF STEIFF'S EARLY BEARS.

LEFT: THE SOFT APPEALING FACIAL FEATURES OF STEIFF'S EARLY TEDDY BEARS ARE ALSO VISIBLE IN THEIR REALISTIC BEARS ON WHEELS. CIRCA 1910.

BELOW: THE RECOGNIZABLE LONG ARMS, BIG FEET, AND HUMP BACK OF STEIFF'S EARLY SHOE-BUTTON EYE BEAR DESIGN CONTINUED TO BE USED WHEN GLASS EYES WERE INTRODUCED IN 1908.

The 1950's are frequently referred to as Steiff's "heyday for exportation." After a dearth of toys during World War II, numerous overseas customers anxiously awaited the beautiful Steiff toys from Germany. Animals circa 1950. *Original Teddy*. Circa 1966.

Three highly collectible Steiff bears from the 1950's. (Left to right) *Jackie*. 13in (33cm); *Zooby*. 11in (28cm); *Baloo*. 14in (36cm). All bears have raised script Steiff buttons.

A magnificent representation of Steiff miniature teddy bears from 1907–1950. *Courtesy Pupenhausmuseum*.

STEIFF *FOUR SEASONS* SERIES. 13IN (33CM); EACH SEASON SOLD
SEPARATELY. LIMITED EDITION STEIFF NORTH AMERICA, INC.
EXCLUSIVE. *COURTESY STEIFF NORTH AMERICA INC.*

STEIFF. *GEORGE*. 2000. 12IN (30CM). THE MOHAIR IS GOLD, WHICH
IS BOTH CELEBRATORY AND TRADITIONAL. GEORGE IS NAMED OF THE
PATRON SAINT OF ENGLAND AND REMAINS A FAVORITE CHRISTIAN
NAME. PRODUCED EXCLUSIVELY FOR TEDDY BEARS OF WITNEY,
GEORGE WAS THE VERY FIRST LIMITED-EDITION TEDDY BEAR TO BE
MADE BY STEIFF IN THE NEW MILLENNIUM.

IN CELEBRATION OF THE MILLENNIUM, STEIFF MADE THE VERY FIRST
MID-YEAR STEIFF CLUB EXCLUSIVE—*YEAR 2000 TEDDY BEAR.*
*COURTESY STEIFF.*

# Hermann Teddy Original

The history of the Gebr. Hermann KG, Teddy-Plüschspielwarenfabrik, began in 1907 when Johann Hermann (1854/1920) decided to manufacture teddy bears. Assisted by members of his family, he started his trade and business in a small workshop at Neufang near Sonneberg in Thuringia, in the former German Democratic Republic (East Germany). He had three sons and three daughters who all energetically helped him to establish his newly found firm.

In 1912, Johann Hermann's eldest son, Bernard, established his own business independent of his father's after serving an apprenticeship in trade and business. He moved to Sonneberg where he founded a small factory employing several men and women who specialized in manufacturing teddy bears and dolls. At that time, Sonneberg was the world's center of toy manufacturing.

Bernard Hermann had four sons, Hellmuth, Artur, Werner and Horst. Hellmuth, after training in his father's business, later established his own company. While the firm was established in Sonneberg, its name was Bernard Hermann. After 1948 in Hirschaid, it continued as the Teddy-Pluschspielwaren-fabrik Gebr. Hermann KG. The three sons of the original founder became partners in this business. When Bernard Hermann died in 1959, his legacy to his sons included a successful and prosperous business that was a famous worldwide factory of fine teddy bears and other plush animals.

A SELECTION OF EARLY HERMANN BEARS. ONE DISTINCT CHARACTERISTIC OF EARLY HERMANN BEARS IS THE SHORT MOHAIR INSET SNOUT. *COURTESY HERMANN TEDDY ORIGINAL.*

In 1990, the company was renamed Hermann Teddy Original. Currently managing the firm are Werner's daughter, Marion Mehling and Artur's daughter, Margit Drolshagen. Another of Artur's daughters, Traudi Mischer, is the chief designer.

Teddy bears have always been the priority of all animals made by Hermann. Beginning in 1920, the company identified their products with a circular hangtag. An identifiable characteristic of early Hermann bear designs is a short mohair inset snout. The bears' torsos were narrow and their arms were shorter and feet smaller than Steiff bears. They were produced with glass eyes and many designs had tipped mohair.

TOP LEFT: HERMANN TEDDY ORIGINAL. *ZODIAC BEARS.* 2001. 12-½IN (32CM); FOUR DIFFERENT COLORS OF MOHAIR: GREEN FOR SPRING, YELLOW FOR SUMMER, BROWN FOR AUTUMN AND WHITE FOR WINTER. INDIVIDUAL SIGNS OF THE ZODIAC ARE STITCHED ONTO FOOTPAD. DESIGNED BY TRAUDI MISCHNER HERMANN. *COURTESY HERMANN TEDDY ORIGINAL.*

LEFT: HERMANN TEDDY ORIGINAL. *TEDDY BEAR SUMMER WIND.* 2001. 14-¾IN; PALE YELLOW MOHAIR; FULLY-JOINTED WOODEN SCOOTER; LIMITED EDITION OF 800. DESIGNED BY TRAUDI MISCHNER HERMANN. *COURTESY HERMANN TEDDY ORIGINAL.*

# Schuco Toy Company

After learning the toy business at Gebruder Bing, Heinrich Muller combined forces with Heinrich Schreyer and formed Schuco in 1912. It survived Hitler and World War II, but eventually it could not compete with the Japanese toy industry. After fifty years, Schuco (an abbreviation for Schreyer and Co.) closed its doors, leaving behind a toy legacy of collectibles still highly prized the world over. Originally noted for its mechanical toys, Schuco bears and animals delighted children by somersaulting and walking. Dressed in non-removable outfits, Schuco bears came primarily in short bristle-type mohair and vibrant colors.

Schuco received the most recognition for its "Yes/No" mechanism, which worked by moving the tail to direct the animal's head in any direction. Early Schuco mechanical bears are closely aligned in designs to those of Gebruder Bing with small facial features, head and ears, a slightly upturned snout, a slim body, straight narrow arms with slightly curved paws, small round feet and shiny shoe button eyes.

THE SCHUCO COMPANY IN GERMANY WAS RENOWNED FOR CREATING BEARS AND ANIMALS WITH INNOVATIVE DESIGNS. BEARS SUCH AS THIS SCHUCO MESSENGER (BELL HOP) HAS A MECHANISM ENCASED IN THE BODY WHICH, WHEN THE BEARS TAIL IS MOVED FROM SIDE TO SIDE OR UP OR DOWN, ACTIVATES THE HEAD TO NOD "YES" OR "NO". *COURTESY CHRISTIE'S.*

**TOP:** INCLUDED IN SCHUCO'S WIDE RANGE OF INNOVATIVE MINIATURE ANIMALS ARE THESE FASCINATING EXAMPLES (CIRCA 1920'S): PERFUME BOTTLES (REMOVING HEAD OF ANIMAL REVEALS A GLASS PERFUME BOTTLE); COMPACTS (REMOVING HEAD OF ANIMAL ALLOWS BODY TO OPEN AND REVEAL COMPACT); AND FLASKS (REMOVING HEAD OF ANIMAL DISCLOSES CORKED GLASS BOTTLE AND ALUMINUM SHOT GLASS). *COURTESY PATRICIA VOLPE PHOTOGRAPH BY JOHN VOLPE.*

**BOTTOM:** SCHUCO "YES/NO" BEARS. (LEFT TO RIGHT) CIRCA 1950; *TRICKY.* 12IN (31CM), 8IN (20CM); CIRCA 1920'S. 14IN (36CM). THE FACES OF THE 1920'S SCHUCO BEARS HAVE LOTS OF APPEAL. HOWEVER, THE CUTE BODY DESIGN OF SCHUCO'S CIRCA 1950 YES/NO BEARS APPEAR TO BE THE MOST POPULAR AMONG MOST COLLECTORS TODAY.

# Gebruder Bing

Founded in 1865 as a tin and kitchenware company, Gebruder Bing is most known for its fine clockwork bears and toys of the early twentieth century. Walking, climbing and tumbling bears made by Bing are prized collector's items today. Mainly covered in short beige or brown mohair, many of the Bing bears were dressed in colorful felt and silk outfits.

Early bears are similar in design to Steiff with shoe button eyes. The design changed around 1920 to a wide head with glass eyes, long arms, large oval feet, long snout with a distinctive nose stitching, a broad smile, and long wavy mohair.

TOP RIGHT: THE GERMAN COMPANY GEBRÜDER BING IS KNOWN FOR THEIR EARLY 1900'S INNOVATIVE MECHANICAL BEARS. (LEFT TO RIGHT) *TUMBLING (ACRO) BEAR. CIRCA 1920. 9-¾IN (25CM). ROLLER-SKATING BEAR. CIRCA 1912. 8IN (20CM). TUMBLING (ACRO) BEAR. CIRCA 1910. 13IN (33CM). ROLLER-SKATING BEAR. CIRCA 1912. 8IN (20CM). PRIVATE COLLECTION.*

BOTTOM LEFT: EARLY GERMAN GEBRÜDER BING BEARS WERE VERY STEIFF-LIKE IN DESIGN. HOWEVER, THEIR ARMS AND BODY ARE "PLUMPER" COMPARED TO A STEIFF BEAR OF THE SAME SIZE. ORIGINALLY THEY CAME WITH A METAL TAG FASTENED TO THEIR RIGHT EAR WITH THE LETTERS G.B.N. (GEBRÜDER BING NURNBERG) AND/OR A METAL BUTTON FASTENED TO THE LEFT SIDE OF THE BODY WITH THE LETTERS G.B.N. (LEFT) CIRCA 1910. 14IN (36CM). (RIGHT) CIRCA 1910. 10IN (25CM). *PRIVATE COLLECTION.*

BOTTOM RIGHT: THE SMALL FEATURES OF BINGS' EARLY BEAR DESIGNS CHANGED CONSIDERABLY IN THE 1920'S AND THEIR BEARS BECAME MORE IMPRESSIVE LOOKING WITH LONG SNOUTS, BIG FEET AND LONGER MOHAIR. ALSO THE EYES WERE CHANGED TO GLASS. (LEFT TO RIGHT) 20IN (51CM) 12IN (30CM) 24IN (61CM).

# British Teddy Bear Manufacturers

Many of the teddy bears sold in England during the early 1900's were imported from Steiff. The increased popularity of bears induced the English toy makers to create their own version of the teddy bear.

## Dean's

The Dean's Rag Book Company Ltd. was formed in London in 1903 to manufacture rag books, cutout doll sheets and pictures albums. The Company grew rapidly with the burgeoning toy industry, but it was not until World War I that Dean's produced their first catalogue containing mohair bears.

In 1922, Dean's began to produce bears using the Dean's logo and they have been an integral part of Dean's ever since. Interestingly, Dean's also became involved in making character merchandise, and in 1930, produced the first ever *Mickey Mouse* toy.

Dean's moved to Pontypool in Wales in 1972, and in 1988, were bought by the husband and wife team of Neil and Barbara Miller. Since then, Dean's have stopped producing toys and now concentrate almost entirely on making high quality collectible bears. The Dean's Collectors Club is one of the most popular in Britain and has 6,000 active members, all of whom receive a free mohair club bear each year.

LEFT: THE COVER OF A TEDDY BEAR RAG BOOK PRODUCED BY DEAN'S IN 1908.

BELOW LEFT: DEANS. *MYCROFT* BEAR PRODUCED IN THE 1930'S IS A REPRESENTATION OF DEAN'S BASIC BEAR DESIGN FROM THIS PERIOD. GOLD MOHAIR WITH GLASS EYES. PURCHASED AT CHRISTIES AUCTION IN 1993. *DISMAL DESMOND DALMATION.* 1926. *COURTESY DEAN'S.*

BELOW RIGHT: DEAN'S *CHARITY BEAR.* 15IN (38CM). A PERCENTAGE OF THE SALES OF EACH BEAR SOLD IS DONATED TO DIABETES UK CHARITY. LIMITED EDITION 1000. *COURTESY DEAN'S.*

# Merrythought Ltd.

Merrythought, the old English word for wishbone, began as a small spinning mill in 1919 in Yorkshire when Mr. W. G. Holmes (the present Managing Director's grandfather) went into partnership with Mr. G. H. Laxton. They started the business to simply manufacture mohair yarn from imported raw materials. It was not until 1930 that Merrythought Ltd. opened with personnel from toy makers Chad Valley and J. K. Farnell.

The traditional teddy bear was in Merrythought's line from the onset. Introduced in the company's 1931 catalog, the bears came in many different sizes with a wide selection of colors of mohair or "art silk plush." They were fully jointed with brown glass eyes, kapok stuffing, a certain design of webbed paw stitching and a wide vertically stitched nose. Although Merrythought has produced many different products, fortunately for the collector the company maintained good identification of its toys over the years.

ABOVE LEFT: MERRYTHOUGHT'S *LITTLE MASTER MISCHIEF* WON THE PRESTIGIOUS TOBY AWARD IN 1992. *COURTESY MERRYTHOUGHT LTD.*

ABOVE RIGHT: FINE EXAMPLE OF A MERRYTHOUGHT ARTIFICAL SILK PLUSH BEAR PRODUCED IN THE 1930S. EARLY MERRYTHOUGHT BEARS SPORTS THE MERRYTHOUGHT IDENTIFICATION BUTTON IN LEFT EAR AND CLOTH LABEL ON FOOT. *COURTESY PUPPENHAUSMUSEUM, BASEL.*

MERRYTHOUGHT *Cheeky* BEARS. CIRCA 1955. 10IN–5IN (25CM–13CM); GOLD MOHAIR; INSET GOLD VELVETEEN SNOUT; GLASS EYES; FULLY JOINTED; SOFT STUFFING. SINCE ITS CREATION IN 1955, *Cheeky* HAS BEEN ONE OF MERRYTHOUGHT'S MOST POPULAR DESIGNS. HE WAS MADE FOR THE 1955 BRITISH TOY FAIR. HIS EXPRESSION PROMPTED A VERY IMPORTANT PERSON TO COMMENT, "ISN'T HE CHEEKY?" AND THE NAME STUCK. HE'S BEEN *Cheeky* EVER SINCE.

A QUOTE FROM MERRYTHOUGHT, "MERRYTHOUGHT PRODUCTS ARE NOT JUST SOFT TOYS. AS SOON AS THEY LEAVE THE SHELF, THEY BECOME PART OF THE FAMILY, A TREASURED COMPANION, A TRUE FRIEND AND SOMEONE WHO IS NEVER FORGOTTEN."

THESE FIVE ADORABLE MERRYTHOUGHT *Cheekies* ARE ALL EXCLUSIVE TO TEDDY BEARS OF WITNEY. *CHEEKY JACK,* 10IN (26CM); *CHEEKY HEART OF GOLD,* 16IN (41CM); *MISTLETOE CHEEKY,* 11IN (28CM); *CHEEKY LITTLE KITTEN ROSE,* 6IN (15CM). ALL BEARS ARE MADE OF HIGH QUALITY MOHAIR IN LIMITED EDITIONS.

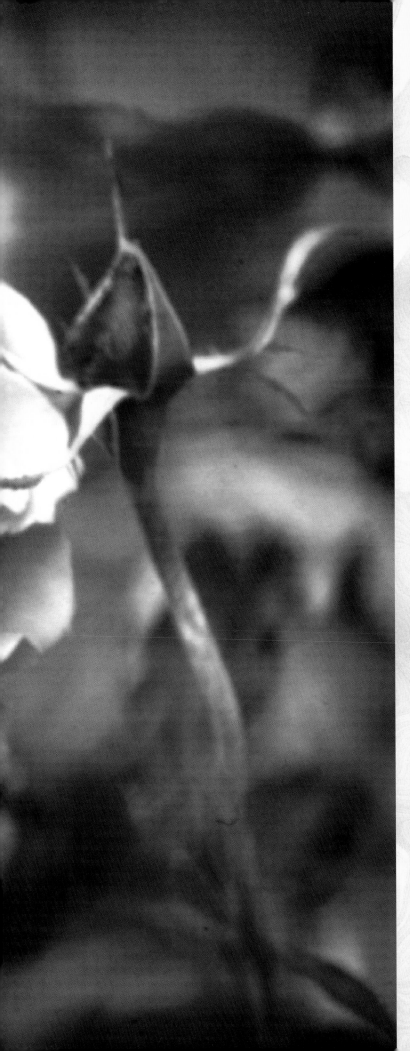

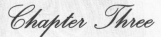

*Chapter Three*

*A Tribute to Teddy Bear Artists*

*The talented efforts of bear artists have made an important impact on the growth of the teddy bear market. The bears lovingly created by bear artists are the antiques of the future. An artist bear is a wonderful piece of sculpture made of fabric and stuffing and filled with love and compassion. One day they will become family heirlooms to enjoy for generations.*

Fabricating handmade teddies has grown from a friendly avocation into a popular cottage industry. The primary home of this unique art form is the United States. However, in my travels I've witnessed handmade teddy bear making rapidly taking hold in Europe, Australia, Japan and a multitude of other countries.

The artists who tell their stories here are pioneers of that elite fraternity of creative people who see the world in artistic terms and are able to express unique feelings with unprecedented freshness and vitality. Artist bear collecting is distinctive in that it welcomes and encourages personal relationships between artists and collectors. Close connections add to the fun and rewards of teddy bear collecting.

## America

### Reinhard Schulte

There has been a close relationship between the manufacture of the first German teddy bears and the originator of mohair plush fabric, Reinhard Schulte. He developed this special fabric in 1901, and over the next 100 years it proved to be the magic of the Steiff Company.

It did not take long for Reinhard Schulte to include a dyeing facility on the premises and begin the unique innovations such as adding different colored tips to the pile for which he became known.

### Elke and Ron Block — Edinburgh Imports

In 1981, Ron and Elke Block established Edinburgh Imports. It became the first company in the world to import increasing varieties of mohair for the general sale to artists and hobbyists. An avid collector and dealer of Steiff, Elke needed fabrics for repair. Steiff was kind enough to give extra fabric to Elke who shared it with her friends. Until then, old coats, blankets or auto seat covers found in thrift stores or flea markets served the artist. Requests to "find more of that great mohair" led Elke and Ron to Schulte. Schulte has now become the benchmark of finest quality mohair plush.

Thrilled artists who used the Blocks' products inspired Ron and Elke to expand their private collection of bears and the variety of mohair fabrics for Edinburgh. They work with artists and companies on five continents and visit a variety of shows every year to keep up-to-date on artists' needs and developments.

RIGHT: REINHARD SCHULTE (RIGHT) LOOKING AT A TEDDY BEAR IN THE HANDS OF PAUL STEIFF. PICTURE WAS TAKEN IN 1908. *COURTESY REINHARD SCHULTE.*

FAR RIGHT: REALIZING THE INCREASING INTEREST IN TEDDY BEAR MAKING IN AMERICA, RON AND ELKE BLOCK BEGAN TO IMPORT THE GERMAN MOHAIR PLUSH FABRICS. TOGETHER, THEY STARTED A FABRIC COMPANY CALLED EDINBURGH IMPORTS NOW IN NEWBURY PARK, CALIFORNIA.

# Pamm Bacon — A Bear To Be Noticed

Pamm started making her own doll clothes before she was ten. Her love of miniatures evolved into the business of making miniature bears with painted accessories or features on the bears themselves.

# Janie Comito — Janie Bear

Janie Comito left a career in graphic design in 1979 to begin making teddy bears. One of the first in the field, she and her husband George have also created teddy inspired photographic art for magazines, slide presentations, cards and books.

TOP LEFT: PAMM BACON, BEAR TO BE NOTICED.

TOP RIGHT: PAMM BACON, BEAR TO BE NOTICED. A REPRESENTATION OF THE FINE ARTWORK THIS TALENTED ARTIST INCORPORATES INTO HER LINE OF MINIATURE BEARS AND BEAR-RELATED ITEMS.

BOTTOM LEFT: JANIE COMITO WITH A GOBLET OF HER EXQUISITE MINIATURE BEADED STRAWBERRY BEAR CREATIONS. PHOTOGRAPH BY GEORGE COMITO.

BOTTOM RIGHT: JANIE COMITO, JANIE BEAR. A DELIGHTFUL ARRAY OF HANDMADE BEADED HATPIN BEARS AND MINIATURE BEARS DECORATE THIS VICTORIAN-STYLE PINCUSHION. BEARS. 1998. 1-½IN–4IN (4CM–10CM). PHOTOGRAPH BY GEORGE COMITO.

## Flore Emory —— Flore Bears

In 1979, Flore started making teddy bears for the children. When grown-ups expressed an interest in them as well, she developed an authentic style of individualistic bears with elongated features and humpbacks. Visitors to her home find bears riding in old wagons or goat carts on the lawn, holding school in the living room or cooking in "Granny's Kitchen."

## Sue & Randall Foskey —— Nostalgic Bears

Sue and Randall's bear making began with a jointed teddy bear for their daughter's Christmas present. After studying the characteristics of antique bears, Sue started drafting her own patterns. By 1985, they were so busy that Randall decided to retire from Chief of Police to travel and make bears full time. The Foskeys designed for Annette Funicello back in the early 1990's.

TOP LEFT: FLORE EMORY ENJOYS THE WARMTH OF THE FIRE IN HER RUSTIC COUNTRY HOME WITH SOME OF HER FAVORITE NOSTALGIC-STYLE BEAR CREATIONS.

TOP RIGHT: THE RURAL COUNTRY SETTING OF FALLBROOK, IN CALIFORNIA'S SAN DIEGO COUNTY IS JUST THE PLACE YOU WOULD IMAGINE FLORE EMORY'S FLORE BEARS WOULD CALL HOME.

BOTTOM LEFT: SUE AND RANDALL FOSKEY, NOSTALGIC BEARS.

BOTTOM RIGHT: SUE AND RANDALL FOSKEY, NOSTALGIC BEARS. *THE GREATEST SHOW ON EARTH.* 1999. CREATED FOR WALT DISNEY WORLD'S ONE-OF-A-KIND TEDDY BEAR AUCTION. *PHOTOGRAPH BY RANDALL FOSKEY.*

# Rosalie Frischmann —— Mill Creek Creations

Rosalie is one of the early bear artists, beginning creating bears in 1983. Her bears and their pets are known for their sweet, childlike expressions, their fine workmanship and beautiful accessories. Well-known around the world, they are featured in many magazines, books, calendars, and greeting cards. In addition to the many original small editions, Rosalie began designing for the Barton's Creek Collection—an affordable line by Gund—in 1999.

# Joanne C. Mitchell —— Family Tree Bears

In 1984, Joanne designed her first bear. Six months later, a local shop in Houston was selling her creations. Family Tree Bears' trademark features include needle sculpted nostril nose, custom-made lead crystal eyes and designed original conformations.

TOP LEFT: ROSALIE FRISCHMAN, MILL CREEK CREATIONS.

TOP RIGHT: ROSALIE FRISCHMAN, MILL CREEK CREATIONS. *THE BEARS DRESS UP LIKE POOH AND FRIENDS.* 2000. SIZES RANGE FROM 16IN–21IN (41CM–53CM); HAND-DYED AND PAINTED MOHAIR; AUSTRIAN CRYSTAL EYES; WIRE ARMATURE; TILTABLE HEADS. ONE-OF-A KIND. SOLD AT WALT DISNEY WORLD 2000 TEDDY BEAR AUCTION FOR $13,000.

BOTTOM LEFT: JOANNE C. MITCHELL, FAMILY TREE BEARS.

BOTTOM LEFT: JOANNE C. MITCHELL, FAMILY TREE BEARS. *THE DIVA MILDRED VON BRUIN.* 2000. 26IN (66CM). ONE-OF-A-KIND. SHE IS THE LAST OF THE DIVA TRILOGY - THREE HOLLYWOOD HAS-BEENS FINDING THEIR PLACE IN THE MODERN WORLD. MILDRED USED TO SPEND HER SUMMERS ON THE RIVIERA BUT NOW PREFERS THE BEACHES OF SOUTHERN FLORIDA. AFTERNOONS ARE SPENT SOAKING UP SUN AND JUICE.

## *Kaylee Nilan — Beaver Valley*

Kaylee indulges a passion for fabric, color and realistic bear design in her studio in the Seattle area. Her signature Beaver Valley creations were first conceived in northern California.

## *Beverly Matteson Port — Beverly Port Originals*

Beverly started creating teddy bears in 1950. Her early work bridged the gap between bears manufactured only as toys for children and the modern age of soft-sculpture teddy bears created as originals for collectors of art and teddy bears. As a pioneer in the field, Beverly's work and educational endeavors are known internationally. Her original bear was exhibited at the Louvre in Paris, France and many of her works are currently on display in museums around the world.

TOP LEFT: KAYLEE NILAN AND HUSBAND JEFF, BEAVER VALLEY.

TOP RIGHT: KAYLEE NILAN, BEAVER VALLEY. BEARS. 1994. *BESSIE.* 37IN (94CM); *MATHEW* (IN PJS). 23IN (58CM); *RUTHERFORD.* 40IN (101CM). BEARS PORTRAY ALL THE FAMOUS BEAVER VALLEY FEATURES: HAND-MADE RESIN MOUTH, CLAWS AND NOSE; GLASS EYES; FLEXIBLE ARMATURE (INTRODUCED INTO THE BEAR WORLD BY BEAVER VALLEY IN 1988).

BOTTOM LEFT: BEVERLY MATTESON PORT, BEVERLY PORT ORIGINALS.

BOTTOM RIGHT: BEVERLY MATTESON PORT, BEVERLY PORT ORIGINALS. *TIME MACHINE TEDDIES* AND *REMEMBEARS.* 4IN–30IN (10CM–76CM); HAND-DYED ANTIQUE AND MODERN MOHAIR. SPECIAL FEATURES: DOUBLE-JOINTED NECKS; FULL BODY ARMATURE; SECRET COMPARTMENTS IN BODIES; MUSICAL OR AUTOMATION MECHANISMS.

# Kimberlee Port — Kimberlee Port Originals

Creating miniature teddy bears since the early 1970's, Kimberlee is the first teddy bear artist to create fully jointed and stuffed miniature bears. Many of her early designs, are now common themes in the bear artist market, such as *Bearterfly* (winged butterfly bear), *Fleur* (flower bear), *Teddy Teddy Tree* (Christmas Tree Bear), and *Santa Bear*.

# John Paul Port - Van Poort Originals

Introduced when he was born into the magical world of teddy bears by his mother Beverly Matteson Port. John Paul designed his first bear in 1976 as an anniversary present for his parents. He now creates artist originals and is an avid collector and renowned appraiser of antique bears.

TOP LEFT: KIMBERLEE PORT, KIMBERLEE PORT ORIGINALS.

TOP RIGHT: KIMBERLEE PORT, KIMBERLEE PORT ORIGINALS. (CENTER) *TEDDY TREE*. 10IN (25CM); GREEN MOHAIR; WORKING BLINKING LIGHTS AND OVER 100 TINY ORNAMENTS HAND-APPLIED TO TREE. A GOLD 1-¼IN (3CM) TEDDY STAR TOPS THE TREE. (LEFT) *KRINGLE JINGLE*. 9IN (23CM); TWO COLORS OF VINTAGE PLUSH BODY; MOHAIR HEAD, PAWS AND FEET; RIBBON AND BEAD DECORATIONS; HAND-APPLIED ORNAMENTS ON CHRISTMAS TREE HAT. VARIOUS OTHER BEARS RANGE IN SIZE FROM 3/4IN–10IN (5CM–25CM).

BOTTOM LEFT: JOHN PAUL PORT, VAN POORT ORIGINALS.

BOTTOM RIGHT: JOHN PAUL PORT, VAN POORT ORIGINALS *LAP ROBE* BEAR. 18IN (46CM); MADE FROM ANTIQUE LAP ROBE WITH MOHAIR HEAD; GERMAN GLASS EYES; FULLY JOINTED. ONE-OF A KIND.

## Steve Schutt — Bear "S"-ence

For over 20 years Steve Schutt has produced an imaginative array of teddy bears that have delighted collectors around the world. From *Bear-a-Saurs* and *Beargoyles* to his hallmark *Beddie-Bye-Teddys* and child-size bears dressed in vintage clothing and accessories, each of his bears radiates a sense of life, innocence and often a quiet dignity. Clarion, Iowa's Teddy Bear Reunion in the Heartland will probably always be associated with his name.

## Denis Shaw — Denis's Den

Venturing into the world of bear artistry in 1985, Denis was the first artist to make bears with the double-jointed neck in 1989. His "quizzy face" design was created in 1987. Now his realistic bears on all fours have taken the bear world by storm.

TOP LEFT: STEVE SCHUTT, BEAR-"S"-ENCE.

TOP RIGHT: STEVE SCHUTT, BEAR-"S"-ENCE. 1999. CHILD-SIZE BEAR DRESSED IN VINTAGE CLOTHING; 36IN (91CM) AND SMALL GIRL BEAR DRESSED IN SIMILAR OUTFIT; 12IN (31CM).

BOTTOM LEFT: DENIS SHAW, DENIS' DEN.

BOTTOM RIGHT: DENIS SHAW, DENIS' DEN. *CHARITY.* 29IN (74CM) AND *LIZBUT, THE LIZARD,* 6IN (15CM). MADE FROM ANTIQUE LAP ROBE AND MOHAIR WITH SYNTHETIC FUR COLLAR.

# Kathleen Wallace —— Stier Bears

When antique teddy bears started to become so costly, Kathleen decided to make her own renditions. This was in 1982. Her family business now makes about 600 bears a year.

# Jeanette Warner —— Nettee Bears

Since 1985, Jeanette's main interest has been teddy bears and the materials needed to create a particular look or theme. She creates a pattern reminiscent of the old German bears, yet with her own original and distinctive look.

TOP LEFT: KATHLEEN WALLACE, STIER BEARS.

TOP RIGHT: KATHLEEN WALLACE, STIER BEARS. 1998. HISTORIC PHILADELPHIANS. (LEFT TO RIGHT) *GEORGE WASHINGTON, MARTHA WASHINGTON, BENJAMIN FRANKLIN* AND *BETSY ROSS*.

BOTTOM LEFT: JEANETTE WARNER, NETTEE BEARS.

BOTTOM RIGHT: JEANETTE WARNER, NETTEE BEARS. *THE NIGHT BEFORE CHRISTMAS*. 2000. *FATHER CHRISTMAS*. 14IN (36CM); *CORGI* AND *KITTY*. 10IN (25CM). ONE-OF-A-KIND.

## *Beverly White —— Happy Tymes Collectibles*

Beverly White chose to lay aside a nursing profession in 1984 to begin a doll business called HAPPY TYMES COLLECTIBLES. The little wooden nursery rhyme dolls gave way to the bruins in 1985 when she lacked the three bears to accompany Goldilocks. Her trademark is an identifying, embroidered accent line attached to the eyes of her bears. She calls them worry lines. She currently develops bear designs for Cooperstown Bears and The Franklin Mint and has also designed for Little Gems and the Annette Funicello Bear Company. In 1998, Beverly launched her own manufactured global designs. She resolutely continues to produce her own hand-made bears, including those special editions of the *Portrait Bears*, one of her two registered trademarks.

## *Joan Woessner —— Bear Elegance Exclusives*

Never having a bear as a child, Joan has made up for it in her adult life. By 1984, Joan designed her own bears and taught teddy bear making classes in her craft store. By 1988, she had so many orders that her husband, Michael, started helping full time, and they have worked together since.

TOP LEFT: BEVERLY WHITE, HAPPY TYMES COLLECTIBLES.

TOP RIGHT: BEVERLY WHITE, HAPPY TYMES COLLECTIBLES. *THE HAPPY TYMES GANG.* 1995. 18IN–30IN (46CM–76CM). SIX PIECE PORTRAIT BEAR GROUP.

BOTTOM LEFT: JOAN WOESSNER, BEAR ELEGANCE EXCLUSIVES. ONE OF JOAN'S MOST DEVOTED FANS IS HER GRANDDAUGHTER, MICHELE.

BOTTOM RIGHT: JOAN WOESSNER, BEAR ELEGANCE EXCLUSIVES. *OUR PET BUNNY.* 1995. BEARS. 10IN (25CM) AND 11IN (28CM). MADE FOR CLARION'S "TEDDY BEARS IN THE HEARTLAND" CHARITY AUCTION.

## Austria
### Renate Hanisch —— Bears from No. 27

One of the most famous of Austrian bear makers, Renate Hanisch quit her job as a science teacher after incidentally dropping into a workshop of a British bear maker in 1995. Her colorful designs as well as her classical bruins are easily recognizable as they are frequently featured in various teddy bear magazines.

## Belguim
### Helga Torfs ——
### Collector's Bears By Helga Torfs

Often working with themes like Native Americans, Eskimos, and dwarf bears, Helga also tries to put each bear in a suitable scene to create the right atmosphere.

TOP LEFT: RENATE HANISCH, BEARS FOR NO. 27.

TOP RIGHT: RENATE HANISCH, BEARS FOR NO. 27. *VALENTINIAN.* 2000.

BOTTOM LEFT: HELGA TORFS, COLLECTOR'S BEARS BY HELGA TORFS.

BOTTOM RIGHT: HELGA TORFS, COLLECTOR'S BEARS BY HELGA TORFS. *BEN* AND *BENJAMIN.* 2000. *BEN* (22IN [56CM]) TEACHES HIS BABY SON *BENJAMIN* (12IN [31CM]) HOW TO FLY.

## Germany

### Marie Robischon —— Robin de Bär

Marie's bears have a traditional look with long arms, humped backs, big feet, long snouts and leather paw pads. She uses not only mohair, but also linen, suede, leather, denim or even horse blankets to make the bears. They are elaborately dressed in antique and vintage fabrics with antique accessories that she finds in markets all over Europe.

## Netherlands

### Jane Humme —— Jane Humme Originals

When Jane made her first bear in 1989, there were no bear shows in The Netherlands. Bear enthusiasts brought bears to show to meetings held by the Dutch Teddy Bear Club. After she shared the first bear she made, Jane started to sell her traditional style bears in 1989.

### Judith Schnog —— Itchy's Den

Most of Judith Schnog's bears can fit in the palm of your hand. Sometimes they are whimsically humorous and other times quite realistic. Itchy's Den bears have been sold since 1995.

### Audie F. Sison —— A Teddy . . . by Audie

In 1990, Audie became an artist bear collector, and by 1995, began making his own original design teddies under the trademark A Teddy. . . by Audie. Even though his bear making is a passionate hobby and not a full-time career, he is still internationally known for traditional, nostalgic teddies.

TOP LEFT: MARIE ROBISCHON, ROBIN DE BÄR

TOP RIGHT: MARIE ROBISCHON, ROBIN DE BÄR. *LITTLE BOY BEAR.* 1999. 20IN (51CM); CINNAMON-COLORED MOHAIR; BLACK GLASS EYES; WOOD WOOL AND PELLET STUFFING; LEATHER PAW PADS; HAND-KNITTED SWEATER; SUEDE TROUSERS; LINEN-TYPE JACKET; CARRYING OLD TOY HORN.

**TOP LEFT:** JANE HUMME, JANE HUMME ORIGINALS.

**TOP RIGHT:** JANE HUMME ADDS A PERSONAL TOUCH TO EACH OF THE TRADITIONAL-STYLE BEARS SHE CREATES IN VARIOUS TYPES OF MOHAIR. THE SIZES RANGE FROM 13IN TO 21IN (33CM–53CM).

**MIDDLE LEFT:** LINDA MULLINS (LEFT) PRESENTS DUTCH ARTIST JUDITH SCHNOG (RIGHT) HER "WEST COAST CRYSTAL TEDDY BEAR ARTIST AWARD" AT LINDA'S JANUARY 2001 TEDDY BEAR SHOW IN SAN DIEGO, CALIFORNIA.

**MIDDLE RIGHT:** JUDITH SCHNOG, ITCHY'S DEN. *POLARBAY WATCH. 2000.* THE SCENE MEASURES 8IN X 8IN (20CM X 20CM). THE MINIA-TURE POLAR BEARS AND SEAL RANGE FROM 1-½IN TO 4IN (4CM–10CM). THE PROPS WERE MADE BY ANTONIO SINANOVITCH. THIS PIECE WON A GOLDEN GEORGE AWARD AT TEDDY BÄR TOTAL SHOW IN HENNEF GERMANY IN 2000.

**BOTTOM LEFT:** AUDIE SISON, A TEDDY . . BY AUDIE. *PHOTOGRAPH BY HO PHI LE.*

**BOTTOM RIGHT:** AUDIE SISON, A TEDDY . . BY AUDIE. *LEILANI.* 2000. 18IN (46CM); GERMAN MOHAIR; GLASS EYES; WAXED NOSE. LIMITED EDITION OF THREE.

# United Kingdom

## Sarah Bird & Alexander Longhi — Cotswold Bears

Sarah and Alexander first became interested in the teddy bear industry when, as freelance designers, they accepted a commission to design and build a teddy bear museum in the Cotswolds. They fell in love with old and modern bears alike and attended a teddy bear course with Linda Graves, a long established English teddy artist. Thus, they began to create bears for the museum and themselves. Finding them to be very popular with collectors, they decided to launch Cotswold Bears in 1996.

TOP: SARAH BIRD AND ALEXANDER LONGHI, COTSWOLD BEARS

BOTTOM: SARAH BIRD AND ALEXANDER LONGHI CREATE A VARIETY OF DESIGNS IN SPECIAL COLLECTIONS FOR THEIR COTSWOLD BEARS ANNUAL COLOR CATALOG.

## John and Maude Blackburn —— Canterbury Bears

John Blackburn and his wife Maude formed Canterbury Bears some 23 years ago. The idea of Canterbury Bears evolved when John, a full time artist, was asked to design one bear, as a special favor for a friend. From this very modest and unassuming request, the business started and has now grown into a worldwide family of bears and friends. Canterbury Bears was named after the beautiful and historical city in which they live. The Canterbury Crest itself was a great honor bestowed by the Mayor of Canterbury, and later by The Lord Mayor of Canterbury. Permission to use of the King Edward crown on the crest was given when the Lord Mayor was appointed to the city.

## Amy Goodrich —— Portobello Bear Co.

Amy works in a traditional way with wooden jointing, wood wool and mixed fiber stuffing, creating mainly one-of-a-kind characters which allows the personality of each character to shine through. She also experiments with hand cross-stitched sampler bears, creating the very fabric with which they are made. This involves transforming vintage chenille, vintage appliqué work and embroidery into the most unique, extravagantly intricate characters due to the level of craftsmanship involved with the making of the fabrics. For the lover of undressed bears, she also works with long luxurious mohair to create wild bears with realistic composition noses and soulful eyes with their distinctive facial markings that just beg to be picked up and hugged!

TOP LEFT: FOR MORE THAN 23 YEARS JOHN AND MAUDE BLACKBURN OF CANTERBURY BEARS HAVE BEEN DELIGHTING COLLECTORS AROUND THE WORLD WITH THEIR QUALITY BEAR CREATIONS AND THEIR WARM FRIENDLY PERSONALITIES.

TOP RIGHT: MAUDE BLACKBURN OF CANTERBURY BEARS CREATED *THE QUEEN MOTHER* BEAR IN 2001 IN HONOR OF HER MAJESTY THE QUEEN MOTHER'S 100TH BIRTHDAY. MAUDE SENT HM QUEEN ELIZABETH THE QUEEN MOTHER, A ONE-OF-A-KIND LARGER VERSION OF THIS BEAR AS A BIRTHDAY GIFT. MAUDE RECEIVED A LETTER ON BEHALF OF HM QUEEN ELIZABETH THE QUEEN MOTHER FROM HER LADY-IN-WAITING, THANKING MAUDE FOR THE "SPLENDID BEAR" SHE SENT TO HER MAJESTY.

BOTTOM LEFT: AMY GOODRICH, PORTOBELLO BEAR CO.

BOTTOM RIGHT: AMY GOODRICH, PORTOBELLO BEAR CO. *LORD KITCHENER.* 1999. 40IN (101CM); WEARING ANTIQUE MILITARY COSTUME.

## Jo Greeno

A wonderful bear artist who began by collecting bears and began making bears a decade ago, Jo Greeno says it is her teaching that makes the most significant contributions to the bear world. By sharing her knowledge, skills and enthusiasm, she has encouraged many men, women and children to discover the magic in making their own bear. For seven years, she has designed patterns for *Teddy Bear Times* magazine and more recently for Edinburgh Imports.

## Elaine Lonsdale —— Companion Bears

Elaine's bears are easily identified because of the unique use of millinery and period clothing. In addition, she works with an artistic combination of colors and fabrics, which has helped to open up a new market for collectors.

TOP LEFT: JO GREENO.

TOP RIGHT: JO GREENO PREFERS TO DO ONE-OF-A-KIND BEARS SINCE SHE CAN'T STAND TO DO THE SAME BEAR OVER AND OVER AGAIN. SHE WANTS TO BE EXCLUSIVE, SO HER BEARS HAVE TO BE JUST RIGHT.

BOTTOM LEFT: ELAINE LONSDALE, COMPANION BEARS.

BOTTOM RIGHT: ELAINE LONSDALE, COMPANION BEARS. (LEFT TO RIGHT) *MARIEANNE*. 4IN (10CM); OLD-STYLE MOHAIR; IRISH LINEN HAT; AND HAND-TINTED COTTON COAT. *ELLA*. 6IN (15CM); HAND-TINTED MOHAIR; SILK VELVET HAT; VINTAGE METALLIC LACE ACCESSORIES. *FLORA*. 5-½IN (14CM); TINTED MOHAIR; ANTIQUE SILK FLOWERS TRIM WIDE-BRIMMED HAT.

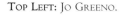

# Sue Quinn —— Dormouse Designs

Sue has designed and created bears and other animals for 35 years, always firmly believing that the small creations were intended for adult enthusiasts. She was one of the very first bear artists in Britain. She is best known for combining a love of antique trimmings and nostalgia with her many characters.

# Paula Strethill-Smith —— Shultz Characters

Shultz Characters recreate the classic traditional old-looking teddy bears in miniature. Paula's career started when she found an antique 1920's Schuco compact bear in 1992. She replicated him into a small mohair teddy bear and began her business, which now includes her husband, Simon, who himself has an exceptional talent for designing pressed felt dolls and characters.

TOP LEFT: SUE QUINN, DORMOUSE DESIGNS.

TOP RIGHT: SUE QUINN, DORMOUSE DESIGNS. *VISITING GRAN.* 2000. 30IN (76CM).

BOTTOM LEFT: PAULA STRETHILL-SMITH, SHULTZ CHARACTERS.

BOTTOM RIGHT: PAULA STRETHILL-SMITH, SHULTZ CHARACTERS. *MASTER JACK.* 1999. 5-½IN (14CM); DRESSED IN RED PAJAMAS.

## *Japan*

### *Kazuko Ichikawa*

After graduating from the art university, Kazuko worked for TAKARA Toy Company where she designed for the Japanese fashion dolls, *Barbie* and *Jenny*. She made her first bear in 1987 and since then, has published three picture books for children and one on how to make Teddy Bears.

TOP: KAZUKO ICHIKAWA

BOTTOM: KAZUKO ICHIKAWA.
*DREAMING IN AFTERNOON*. 1998.
TWO GIRLS PLAYING AND WHISPERING
IN A BEAUTIFUL FOREST.

## *Ikuyo Kasuya — Bruin*

Making teddy bears since 1980, Ikuyo has since been spreading the joy and the pleasure of teddy bears by exhibiting, teaching how to make bears, publishing and appearing on TV.

## *Mari and Akemi Koto — Koto Bears*

This mother and daughter have been making teddy bears for 17 years since Mari was introduced to teddy bears as a piano student in Europe. Akemi is a professor of Kimono making. The two work together to make their own line of bears.

TOP LEFT: IKUYO KASUYA, BRUIN. *PHOTOGRAPH BY HIDEDKI HDYDSHI.*

TOP RIGHT: IKUYO KASUYA, BRUIN. BEARS. 12IN (30CM). *PHOTOGRAPH BY HIDEDKI HDYDSHI.*

BOTTOM LEFT: MARI (LEFT) AND AKEMI (RIGHT) KOTO, KOTO BEARS.

BOTTOM RIGHT: MARIE AND AKEMI KOTO, KOTO BEARS. *A GOOD FRIEND.* 2000. (LEFT) *MARGARET.* (RIGHT) *DAISY.* 18IN (46CM);. CREATED FOR WALT DISNEY WORLD'S 2000 ONE-OF-A-KIND TEDDY BEAR AUCTION.

## *Hiro Takahashi — Fairy Chuckle*®

His wife, teddy bear artist Michi Takahashi, influenced Japan's first male Teddy Bear Artist, Hiro Takahasi. Completing his first bear in 1991, his work has now evolved to that of miniature bears.

## *Michi Takahashi — Fairy Chuckle*®

One of the pioneers, Michi is a highly regarded artist from her country whose work is extremely collectible. She has been creating endearing bears since 1988 under the *Fairy Chuckle*® label. She is completely self-taught, and her bear designs are entirely stitched by hand. Over the years she has created many one-of-a-kind special pieces for prestigious museums in Japan and England as permanent displays. In 2001, she and her husband, Hiro, opened their own museum, Michi & Hiro Takahashi's World, Hakodate Meiji-kan (built in 1911).

TOP LEFT: HIRO TAKAHASHI, FAIRY CHUCKLE®. PHOTOGRAPH BY MAMORU MATSUZAKI.

TOP RIGHT: HIRO TAKAHASHI, FAIRY CHUCKLE®. *MOTHER AND COY CUBS IN HUDSON BAY*©. 2000. 16IN LONG X 8IN HIGH (41CM X 20CM). PHOTOGRAPH BY MITSUYASU SHIMIZU.

BOTTOM LEFT: MICHI TAKAHASHI, FAIRY CHUCKLE®. PHOTOGRAPH BY MAMORU MATSUZAKI.

BOTTOM RIGHT: MICHI TAKAHASHI, FAIRY CHUCKLE®. *THE GRACIOUS BANQUET*. 1998 - 2000. (LEFT TO RIGHT) *SAKURA, MOE, CHRISTINE, CHITOSE* AND *AKANE*. 22IN (56CM). PHOTOGRAPH BY MITSUYASU SHIMIZU.

## Mayumi Watanabe — Mammie Bear © 1990

When her father, an antique toy collector gave her an old Steiff bear, Mayumi was inspired to make teddy bears herself. She utilized her sewing, embroidery and design talents and started her career as a teddy bear artist under the trade name of Mammie Bear in 1990. The distinctive feature of Mammie Bear is its classical design reminiscent of the old German bears made in the early 1900's. As a television producer, Mayumi also plans and produces many TV programs on teddy bears.

## Terumi Yoshikawa — Terumi Bear/Rose Bear

Since seeing her first British antique teddy bear in 1988, Terumi has created about 3,000 teddy bears for adoption at home and in other countries. Her first bears showed Japanese customs, culture and national sports. Later teddy bears depicted celebrities and famous people in history.

TOP LEFT: MAYUMI WATANABE, MAMMIE BEAR© 1990.

TOP RIGHT: MAYUMI WATANABE, MAMMIE BEAR. © 1990. *TWO CUBS PLAYING WITH THEIR PARENT. DANIEL* (PARENT) 16IN (41CM). *KERRY* (CUBS) 8IN (20CM).

BOTTOM LEFT: TERUMI YOSHIKAWA, ROSE BEAR.

BOTTOM RIGHT: TERUMI YOSHIKAWA, ROSE BEAR. (TOP) *PINE*. 1995. 19IN (48CM). (BOTTOM) SURFER BEAR WITH PINEAPPLE HAIR STYLE.

Chapter Four

*The*

*Teddy Bear Scene*

# Teddy Bear Museums

## Teddy Bear Museum of Naples — Florida, USA

The Teddy Bear Museum opened in Naples Florida on December 19, 1990 after the Museum's founder, Frances Pew Hayes (Frannie), donated 1,500 bear items. A decade later, the museum bears range from one-inch to bigger than life! Bears from all over the world are exhibited in this most unusual museum. Bears made of fabric, marble, crystal, wood and bronze, in every shape and size represent the world's most imaginative bear designers and are ready to delight the young at heart no matter what the age. The friendly bears, staff and volunteers at the Teddy Bear Museum greet more than 40,000 visitors every year from around the world.

TOP: BEAR SCULPTURES ENHANCE THE BEAUTIFUL SETTING OF THE TEDDY BEAR MUSEUM OF NAPLES, FLORIDA. *COURTESY TEDDY BEAR MUSEUM OF NAPLES.*

RIGHT: MORE THAN 4,000 TEDDY BEARS WAIT TO CHARM THE HEART OF EVERYONE WHO VISITS THE TEDDY BEAR MUSEUM OF NAPLES. *COURTESY TEDDY BEAR MUSEUM OF NAPLES.*

# Puppenhausmuseum — Basel, Switzerland

Gigi Oeri, owner and founder of the Puppenhausmuseum, has always been inspired by visits to the Basle autumn fair and attracted to the miniature world. More than 20 years ago, an old carrousel became the cornerstone of her growing collection that includes precious doll's houses and shops. When a marvelous four-story house at No.1 Steinenvorstadt went on sale in the mid- 1990's, a project quickly took shape that had been lying dormant in her mind for many years. Together with her husband Andreas Oeri, Gigi founded the privately funded, non-profit-making Steineck Foundation. The 1867 building was successfully converted and in the spring of 1998, was finally opened in the heart of Basle. Those who come to the Puppenhausmuseum can let their imagination run free as there are an amazing number of items to admire in the 1,000+ square meters of the museum.

TOP LEFT: GIGI OERI, WITH THE HELP OF HER HUSBAND ANDREAS OERI, OPENED THE *PUPPENHAUSMUSEUM* IN THE SPRING OF 1998 IN THE HEART OF BASEL, SWITZERLAND. *COURTESY PUPPENHAUSMUSEUM.*

TOP RIGHT: EARLY 1900'S STEIFF TEDDY BEAR AND DOLL HOUSE USED FOR THE *PUPPENHAUSMUSEUM* LOGO. *COURTESY PUPPENHAUSMUSEUM.*

BOTTOM LEFT: THE *PUPPENHAUSMUSEUM* HOUSES ONE OF THE LARGEST AND FINEST REPRESENTATIONS OF RARE AND COLLECTIBLE STEIFF TEDDY BEARS. THIS ENDEARING PAIR ARE *PETSY* BEARS MADE IN 1928/1929. RIGHT IS A NEVER-PRODUCED PROTOTYPE. SIZES (RIGHT) 13-¾IN (35CM), (LEFT) 12-½IN (32CM). *COURTESY PUPPENHAUSMUSEUM.*

BOTTOM RIGHT: VISITING THE *PUPPENHAUSMUSEUM* PROMOTES FREE IMAGINATION. THE MINIATURIZED INTERIORS ALTERNATE WITH SPACIOUS SCENERY AND IS INHABITED WITH TEDDY BEARS FROM THE MOST REPUTABLE MANUFACTURERS. *COURTESY PUPPENHAUSMUSEUM.*

# Teddy Bear Kingdom — Nagasaki, Japan

Huis ten Bosch, one of Asia's largest resorts/theme parks located in Nagasaki, Japan, opened Teddy Bear Kingdom and Linda teddy bear specialty shop on October 10, 1997. The public response was overwhelming and more than a million people toured the museum in one year. The museum is housed in a 1,300 square foot replica of a Dutch castle constructed near the entrance of the theme park. Here, visitors from around the world can see the finest examples of teddy bear history including the growth of its popularity. There are 1,500 various categories of bears on exhibit. Attractive vignettes line the hallways representing rare, unusual and appealing antique bears from 1904 through to the 1960's. As antique bears are almost non-existent in Japan, these exhibits give the visitors a rare opportunity to view bears they otherwise would never see.

Over 40 renowned international artists were invited to create one-of-a-kind display pieces for the artists' bear room in the theme of "Family." With each exhibit the artists were asked to portray something significant about their country's culture and/or history. Teddy Bear Kingdom is another magnificent example in the chain of global commitments from the bear community to extend the magical power of the teddy bear around the world.

THE REGAL AND ELEGANT KASTEEL (CASTLE) NIJENRODE, AT THE ENTRANCE TO HUIS TEN BOSCH BECAME HOME OF THOUSANDS OF TEDDY BEARS FROM ALL OVER THE WORLD. TEDDY BEAR KINGDOM OPENED ON OCTOBER 10, 1997 AND IS COMMITTED TO SHOWCASING THE FINE ART AND HISTORY OF TEDDY BEARS. *COURTESY HUIS TEN BOSCH.*

RIGHT: A TEDDY BEAR COLLECTOR'S HOME CAN BE A FUN PLACE TO VISIT. THIS ROOM IN TEDDY BEAR KINGDOM IS A REPLICA OF ITS HONORARY DIRECTOR, LINDA MULLINS' TEDDY BEAR ROOM. *COURTESY HUIS TEN BOSCH.*

BELOW: IN ACCORDANCE WITH THE ATMOSPHERE OF THE CASTLE, IT WAS DECIDED TO HAVE LIFE-SIZED BEARS REPRESENT A DUTCH ROYAL FAMILY WHO LIVED IN THE CASTLE. AMERICAN ARTISTS JOAN WOESSNER AND STEVE SCHUTT CREATED THE ROYAL FAMILY OF BEARS EXHIBITED AT THE ENTRANCE OF TEDDY BEAR KINGDOM. *COURTESY HUIS TEN BOSCH.*

LINDA MULLINS, HONORARY DIRECTOR OF TEDDY BEAR KINGDOM, POSES FOR A PICTURE WITH BILLY, TEDDY BEAR KINGDOM'S LOGO BEAR, IN FRONT OF TEDDY BEAR SHOP LINDA.

BELOW: THE MAGIC OF THE CIRCUS IS DEPICTED IN THIS HUGE MECHANICAL EXHIBIT IN ONE OF THE MANY INTERESTING DISPLAYS WITHIN TEDDY BEAR KINGDOM. *COURTESY HUIS TEN BOSCH.*

SINGAPOREAN TEDDY BEAR ARTIST FABIAN SONG CREATED THIS MAGNIFICENT BEAR FOR EXHIBITION IN TEDDY BEAR KINGDOM. *CHU BA WANG* IS 23IN (58CM) TALL AND IS DRESSED TO REPRESENT A PARAGON OF A CHINESE CULTURAL DANCE DRAMA CHARACTER.

# Yoshihiro Sekiguchi's Teddy Bear Museums — Izu, Nasu and Hakone, Japan

Yoshihiro Sekiguchi is the founder of the Izu, Nasu and Hakone teddy bear museums, in Japan. Mr. Sekiguchi's first encounter with the teddy bear was in the late 1970's. He was strongly impressed by its unique beauty, the comfort it provided, and how it has captivated the hearts of people all over the world since its creation.

He acquired the famous *Teddy Girl* and *Teddy Edward* for his museums in addition to other special antique manufactured and artist teddy bears. The first museum to open was the Izu Museum in April of 1995. Home to 2,000 bears, this beautiful wooden two-storied structure was inspired by the gracious manor houses of England. This was the first full-scale teddy bear museum to open in Japan. After its tremendous success, Mr. Sekiguchi opened the Nasu museum in July 1997 and then the Hakone museum in July 1999.

TOP LEFT: YOSHIHIRO SEKIGUCHI PROUDLY HOLDS *TEDDY GIRL*, ONE OF THE MOST TREASURED BEARS IN HIS IZU TEDDY BEAR MUSEUM. *TEDDY GIRL* SOLD FOR MORE THAN $170,000 AT CHRISTIE'S SOUTH KENSINGTON AUCTION IN LONDON. IT WAS ORIGINALLY OWNED BY COL. BOB HENDERSON AND SEEMS VERY HAPPY IN HER NEW HOME IN JAPAN. *COURTESY YOSHIHIRO SEKIGUCHI.*

TOP RIGHT: LINDA AND WALLY MULLINS WERE FASCINATED BY THE HUGE MECHANICAL TALKING BEAR THAT GREETS EVERYONE AT THE ENTRANCE TO THE IZU TEDDY BEAR MUSEUM.

BOTTOM: A TEDDY BEAR FACTORY IS AT THE CENTER OF THE IZU MUSEUM. THIS HUGE MECHANICAL EXHIBIT PORTRAYS THE VARIOUS STAGES OF A BEAR UNDER PRODUCTION. EACH BEAR IS APPROXIMATELY 10IN (25CM) TALL. *COURTESY YOSHIHIRO SEKIGUCHI.*

# Cheju Teddy Bear Museum — Korea

The museum owner and founder, Mr. Jesse Kim, is also the founder of J. S. International, Inc. This sixteen-year-old company manufactures more than 10 million plush toys each year. Having collected teddy bears for about six years, Mr. Kim was charmed by their virtue. He decided to return some of his company's profits from the toy business by investing to build a quality teddy bear museum in Korea. Mr. Kim estimates 300,000 visitors per year will visit his museum. On May 5, 2001 National Children's Day—6,100 people visited the museum! The Cheju Teddy Bear Museum is located on the island of Cheju, in Korea. The grand opening of the museum was April 22, 2001. The total floor space is about 700 square meters (approximately 7,500 square feet) with 3 floors housing 2 display rooms (700 square meters). Total area surrounding the museum is about 14,500 square meters. The Cheju Museum is considered a small theme park for family members to enjoy rather than a typical museum focused on valuable treasures securely displayed inside the building.

The museum only showcases bears, no other dolls or toys. There are about 100 individual exhibits housing approximately 1,000 teddy bears including artist, antique, and manufactured plush teddy bears. Mr. Kim's personal teddy bear collection will be on exhibit in the museum. One of the special and most famous bears in the museum is his Steiff *Louis Vuitton Bear*. Mr. Jesse Kim, owner of Cheju museum paid a world-record price of $193,477 for this precious one-of-kind bear.

MR. JESSE KIM (RIGHT) PROUDLY HOLDS HIS NEW TEDDY BEAR, *LOUIS VUITTON.* THIS SPECIAL ONE-OF-A-KIND BEAR WAS MADE BY STEIFF AND DRESSED BY MARIA-LUISA DE LORENZO IN HOMAGE TO HER GRANDFATHER, A STUDENT AT THE ECOLE DES ARTISTES DE PARIS AND A DESIGNER AT DIOR AT THE BEGINNING OF THE LAST CENTURY. SHE USED 1930'S FAILLE SILK FOR THE HAND-EMBROIDERED CAP AND 1904 BACCARAT CRYSTAL SAUVAGE BUTTONS AND BRAID FROM THE SAME PERIOD. MR. KIM WAS THE SUCCESSFUL BIDDER FOR THIS MAGNIFICENT BEAR AT A CHARITY TEDDY BEAR AUCTION IN MONTE CARLO TO BENEFIT THE NEEDY AND SICK CHILDREN IN AFRICA. MR. KIM PAID A RECORD SETTING PRICE OF $193,477 FOR THIS PRECIOUS BEAR. THE BEAR WILL BE SHOWCASED IN MR. KIM'S MAGNIFICENT NEW TEDDY BEAR MUSEUM IN CHEJU, KOREA. STANDING TO THE LEFT ON THIS PICTURE IS MR. BERNHARD M. RÖSNER, MANAGING DIRECTOR OF MARGARETE STEIFF GMBH. *COURTESY CHEJU TEDDY BEAR MUSEUM.*

**ABOVE:** THE CHEJU TEDDY BEAR MUSEUM IN KOREA OPENED ON APRIL 22, 2001. THE CENTER OF THE MUSEUM IS A HUGE GLASS CONE. THIS IS THE FIRST TIME A STRUCTURE OF THIS TYPE WAS ATTEMPTED IN KOREA. *COURTESY CHEJU TEDDY BEAR MUSEUM.*

**LEFT:** THE CHEJU TEDDY BEAR MUSEUM'S *TIME TRAVELER BEAR*, WAS CREATED BY AMERICAN ARTIST BEVERLY WHITE. THE TIME TRAVELER BEAR TAKES THE MUSEUM VISITORS ON A VISUAL TRIP BACK THROUGH THE DECADES OF THE 20TH CENTURY. THE MUSEUM'S SERIES OF "DECADE DIORAMAS", COMMEMORATE TEN EVENTS OF WORLDWIDE INTEREST AND PROGRESS IN THE 20TH CENTURY.

# Teddy Bear Collectors

People are experiencing the joys of teddy bear collecting worldwide. Some collectors choose to specialize in certain types of bears, certain manufacturers, or certain artists. Others are enthralled by almost anything related to bears. As with other collectibles such as stamps, coins, books, or rare toys, you cannot fully enjoy your collection of teddy bears without becoming knowledgeable of its character and history. It requires study and self–education, but ultimately your hobby will become more satisfying and rewarding. Clubs, shows, books, magazines, and the Internet are just a few of the avenues that will enhance your love and interest in one of the world's most popular collectibles, the Teddy Bear.

TOP LEFT: BILL BOYD, AT THE TOY AND MINIATURE MUSEUM OF KANSAS CITY, MISSOURI, HOLDING A BASKET WITH HIS TWO FAVORITE BEARS – *GULLIVER JUNIOR* BY ARTIST CINDY ANSHUTZ, AND *LITTLE GULLIVER,* STEIFF'S RENDITION OF CINDY ANSHUTZ ORIGINAL *GULLIVER.* THE MUSEUM PURCHASED THE ORIGINAL *GULLIVER* AT THE GOOD BEARS OF THE WORLD JUBILEE AUCTION IN 1999 GARNERING $6,000 FOR GOOD BEARS OF THE WORLD'S BEAR BANK.

TOP RIGHT: STEVE ESTES WITH TWO OF HIS PRIMARY INTER-ESTS, MUSIC AND TEDDY BEARS. (LEFT TO RIGHT) *JOHNATHAN.* STEIFF. CIRCA 1908. 28IN (71CM); STEIFF. CIRCA 1907. 16IN (41CM); *TUG.* STEIFF. 1907. 20IN (51CM); "CENTER SEAM" IN HEAD. *PHOTOGRAPH BY ALVIN GEE.*

BOTTOM: CHUCK STEFFES AND HIS WIFE CATHY ARE AVID BEAR COLLECTORS. AMONG THEIR MANY FAVORITES ARE EARLY STEIFF AND BING BEARS.

# Teddy Bear Stores

Most teddy bear stores are operated by bear lovers who conduct business with a special attitude. Their promotion of teddy bear collecting as a joyous experience makes their shops cozy and friendly typically featuring top quality merchandise, fair prices and personalized one-on-one fair service. Each seems to have its own unique atmosphere reflecting the personality of its proprietors. Stop into any one of the hundreds of these quaint shops around the world and you're bound to be caught up in the magic of the teddy bear.

TOP: MARIE BALSA SAYS THE SUCCESS OF HER TEDDY BEAR STORE, MY FRIENDS AND ME, IS DUE TO THE COMFORTABLE, RELAXED, COZY SETTING SHE CREATES FOR HER COLLECTORS.

BOTTOM: EACH YEAR, MARIE BALSA CONDUCTS AN ANNIVERSARY PARTY IN CELEBRATION OF THE 1984 OPENING OF MY FRIENDS AND ME. SEVERAL OUTSTANDING ARTISTS ARE INVITED FROM AROUND THE WORLD FOR A PERSONAL APPEARANCE. TYPICALLY, THESE PARTIES DRAW ENTHUSIASTS FROM AROUND THE COUNTRY. IN CELEBRATION OF HER 15TH ANNIVERSARY, MARIE (CENTER RIGHT) INVITED (LEFT TO RIGHT) GREGORY GYLLENSHIP, MARY ANN WILLS, AND AUDIE SISON.

**TOP LEFT:** BETH AND BEN SAVINO JOINED BETH'S FAMILY BUSINESS, HOBBY CENTER TOYS, IN THE MID-1970'S. TODAY THESE TWO ARDENT BEAR, DOLL AND TOY COLLECTORS OWN THE TOY STORE IN THE FRANKLIN PARK MALL, TOLEDO, OHIO.

**TOP RIGHT:** BARRIE SHAPIRO, OWNER OF THE TOY SHOPPE IN RICHMOND, VIRGINIA, SPENDS HOURS AT THE COMPUTER MAKING SURE HER COLLECTORS ARE INFORMED OF THE LATEST AND MOST POPULAR COLLECTIBLE BEARS AND DOLLS ON THE MARKET.

**BOTTOM:** IAN POUT IN FRONT OF HIS WORLD-FAMOUS SHOP TEDDY BEARS OF WITNEY IN OXFORDSHIRE, ENGLAND. STANDING WITH HIM ARE THREE OF HIS INVALUABLE STAFF (LEFT TO RIGHT) JANICE, GINA AND LIZ.

TOP LEFT: MARGARET AND GERRY GREY, OWNERS OF THE TEDDY BEAR SHOP IN NORTHANTS, ENGLAND, ARE BASICALLY TEDDY BEAR COLLECTORS AT HEART WHOSE HOBBY GOT A LITTLE OUT OF HAND!

TOP RIGHT: THE LATE PAM HEBBS IS CONSIDERED TO BE ONE OF THE GREAT PIONEERS OF THE MODERN TEDDY BEAR MOVEMENT. HER TINY MAGICAL SHOP IN CAMDEN PASSAGE, ONE OF LONDON'S FAMOUS ANTIQUE MARKETS, WAS A COLLECTOR'S PARADISE PACKED FULL OF TEDDY BEARS AND TEDDY BEAR MEMORABILIA.

BELOW: MARGARET AND GERRY GREY FEEL A SERIOUS IMPACT WAS MADE AND BRITISH TEDDY BEAR ARTISTRY REALLY BEGAN AT THEIR FIRST INTERNATIONAL TEDDY BEAR MASTER CLASS GIVEN BY INVITED TOP AMERICAN ARTISTS JOAN WOESSNER AND STEVE SCHUTT IN 1991.

# *Teddy Bear Dealers*

Reputable teddy bear dealers frequently get their start as collectors and begin dealing in bears to satisfy their own love of these wonderful creatures. They frequently share their knowledge by giving lectures and presentations and writing for magazines all the while learning more and more about bears. Most feel that a knowledgeable collector is a better one, and as a dealer, they are pleased to answer any questions from novice and experienced collectors. Today, many dealers include the Internet as a method of advertising and selling bears. You can frequently find just what you're looking for by going "online."

TOP: TEDDY BEAR DEALER DOTTIE AYERS HAS SPECIALIZED IN ANTIQUE STEIFF TEDDY BEARS, ANIMALS AND DOLLS SINCE 1980. *COURTESY DOTTIE AYERS.*

BOTTOM: DOTTIE AYERS WAS DELIGHTED TO DISCOVER THIS 1940 STEIFF DISPLAY PIECE STORED IN THE BASEMENT OF A TOY STORE IN RICHMOND, VIRGINIA. *STEIFF VILLAGE WITH BELL TOWER.* CIRCA LATE 1940'S. 36IN DEEP X 48IN WIDE X 41IN TALL (91CM X 122CM X 104CM). A WEDDING PARTY OF 22 STEIFF ANIMALS ROTATE AROUND IN A CIRCLE. A *ZOTTY* BEAR PHOTOGRA-PHER SNAPS PICTURES AS THEY GO BY. THREE BEARS DANCE ROUND AND ROUND THE TOP DECK. THE STEIFF ANIMALS INCLUDE ORIGINAL TEDDIES, TWO LARGE AND TWO SMALL TEDDY BABIES, DUCK, PANDA, SCOTTIE DOG AND TWO *ZOTTIES.* THE MAJORITY OF THE ANIMALS HAVE RAISED SCRIPT BUTTONS, STOCK TAGS AND US ZONE LABELS. *COURTESY DOTTIE AYERS.*

TOP LEFT: BARBARA BALDWIN SHOWN HERE WITH A REPRESENTATION OF THE MAGNIFICENT AND RARE ANTIQUE TEDDY BEARS THAT HAVE PASSED THROUGH HER HANDS OVER THE 25 YEARS. SHE SPECIALIZES IN ANTIQUE TEDDY BEARS, ANIMALS AND RELATED ITEMS. (LEFT TO RIGHT) EDUARD CRÄMER. CIRCA 1930'S. 20IN (51CM); GREEN-TIPPED MOHAIR. STEIFF. CIRCA 1905. 18IN (46CM); APRICOT MOHAIR; BLANK BUTTON. BING. CIRCA 1920'S. 24IN (61CM); BEIGE WAVY MOHAIR.

BOTTOM LEFT: LONG TIME TEDDY BEAR DEALER AND COLLECTOR DAVID DOUGLAS WITH TWO OF HIS FAVORITE EARLY "CENTER SEAM" STEIFF BEARS.

TOP RIGHT: OVER THE YEARS BARBARA BALDWIN'S DAUGHTER, JESSICA, HAS POSED FOR PICTURES WITH SOME WONDERFUL BEARS AND ANIMALS. THIS IS JESSICA AT SIX YEARS OLD WITH A 28IN (71CM) REGINA BROCK ARTIST BEAR AND A STEIFF STUDIO GOOSE. *COURTESY BARBARA BALDWIN.*

BOTTOM RIGHT: LIVING IN GERMANY GIVES ANTIQUE TEDDY BEAR COLLECTOR AND DEALER DAVID DOUGLAS THE OPPORTUNITY TO FIND RARE AND WONDERFUL STEIFF TREASURES. THESE TWO MAGNIFICENT, EXTREMELY RARE STEIFF *DICKY* BEARS, 12IN (31CM) AND 14IN (36CM), WERE MADE IN 1933. IN GERMAN, *DICKY* MEANS CHUBBY. *COURTESY DAVID DOUGLAS.*

**TOP LEFT:** A WIDE ARRAY OF RARE EARLY GERMAN AND AMERICAN TEDDY BEARS CAN BE FOUND AT BARBARA LAUVER'S SALES BOOTH AT TEDDY BEAR EVENTS.

**BOTTOM LEFT:** DONNA HARRISON WEST WITH HER TWO PET NORWICH TERRIERS IS SURROUNDED BY SOME OF HER FAVORITE ARTIST AND ANTIQUE BEARS. *COURTESY DONNA HARRISON WEST.*

**TOP RIGHT:** BARBARA LAUVER HAS DELIGHTED HER COLLECTORS, FRIENDS AND RELATIVES BY PHOTOGRAPHING HER RARE EARLY STEIFF BEARS EACH YEAR FOR HER CHRISTMAS CARD.

**BOTTOM RIGHT:** DONNA HARRISON WEST FEELS DRESSING HER ANTIQUE BEARS IS NOT ONLY FUN BUT ALSO GIVES THE BEAR CHARACTER.

# Teddy Bear Auctions

Teddy bears gaining the most recognition, publicity and record-breaking prices during the past decade come from teddy bear auctions. In the past, antique teddy bears did not command high enough prices to be auctioned individually and so would be sold as odd lots or accompanied by an antique doll. Now they have come into their own. Bears made by teddy bear artists have rightfully found a place in the collectible marketplace. Artists worked hard to establish their work as an art form. A one-of-kind artist bear made by a well-known teddy bear artist can command several thousands of dollars at auctions. Teddy bear charity auctions are becoming increasingly more popular all over the world with the majority of them featuring artist designed bears and/or manufactured bears. Thousands of dollars are raised through the continued generosity and the caring nature of these wonderful people. What better way to share the warmth of the teddy bear as goodwill ambassador to all corners of the globe.

## Berryman's International Teddy Bear Artists Auction —— Japan

Berryman's International Teddy Bear Artists Auction was an international effort designed to raise funds by auctioning donated teddy bears. Its goal was to aid those who suffered from the tragic earthquake in Japan (January 17, 1995). Some of the best-known and most caring people in the teddy bear world also joined me to work on this worthy cause. My friends who joined me in this project include Gary Ruddell, publisher of Hobby House Press and Kazundo Onozoka, founder of the Japan Teddy Bear Association (JTBA). Teddy bear artists from all over the world donated 131 one-of-a-kind teddy bears. JTBA organized the touring exhibition of those teddy bears before the auction.

An event of this nature was never before held in Japan. The auction took place January 30, 1996 at the beautiful Tokyo Prince Hotel and raised 22 million yen (approximately $220,000) that was donated to the Japanese Society of Pediatric Psychiatry, doctors who specialize in treating child victims.

Berryman's International Teddy Bear Artist Auction was "Proof Positive of Teddy Bear Power." Approximately $220,000 was raised from 130 donated artist bears. The proceeds were to benefit the 1995 Kobe, Japan earthquake victims. Clifford Berryman Bear® made by American artist Gisele Nash.

Japanese teddy bear artists Mari and Akemi Koto created this magnificent piece—*Kabuto Bear Akira* (which means Saga City in Japanese) as their donation to Berryman's International Teddy Bear Artists Auction. The piece commanded a realized price of $2,000.

*The Zucker Fire Department.* 1995 10in–20in (25cm–51cm). Ready to fight any of the fires of Kobe. The Zucker Fire Department was created and donated by Barbara Sixby to Berryman's International Teddy Bear Artists Auction, to benefit the Kobe earthquake victims. The set commanded a realized price of $3,000.

# Broadway Bears Auction

Scott Stevens originated the Broadway Bears Auction in 1997 when he returned from touring with *Cabaret*. It began as a one-time event with Broadway Cares/Equity Fights AIDS as the beneficiary. Since then, the event has gathered national attention and sponsorship. It features one-of-a-kind bears in theatre costume recreations. The bears are *Bare Bears* from North American Bear Co. Inc. and they are transformed into characters like Gypsy Rose Lee, Marcel Marceau, and dozens of other stars and characters from Broadway. Average bids for these terrifically dressed bears are in the area of $2,000. The auction reliably raises over $100,000 each time it is held.

TOP LEFT: *A CHORUS LINE*, A BEAR FROM BROADWAY BEARS I AUCTION (1998) IS THE TOP-SELLING BEAR TO DATE, COMMANDING AN AUCTION PRICE OF $11,000. *COURTESY BROADWAY CARES*.

TOP RIGHT: BERNADETTE PETERS FROM *ANNIE GET YOUR GUN* HOLDS THE BEAR WEARING AN EXACT REPLICA OF THE COSTUME SHE WEARS IN THE SHOW. *COURTESY BROADWAY CARES. PHOTOGRAPH BY ROBERT MILAZZO PHOTOGRAPHY.*

BOTTOM LEFT: SCOTT STEVENS WITH CHITA RIVERA HOLDING THE BEARS FROM *KISS OF THE SPIDER WOMAN* AND *WEST SIDE STORY. COURTESY BROADWAY CARES. PHOTOGRAPH BY ROBERT MILAZZO PHOTOGRAPHY.*

BOTTOM RIGHT: HOWARD McGILLIN (CURRENT STAR OF *PHANTOM OF THE OPERA* ON BROADWAY) AT THE BROADWAY BEARS IV AUCTION ON FEBRUARY 11, 2001 HOLDING UP THE *PHANTOM OF THE OPERA* BEAR, WHICH SOLD FOR $4,500. *COURTESY BROADWAY CARES. PHOTOGRAPH BY ROBERT MILAZZO PHOTOGRAPHY.*

# Christie's South Kensington Auction House —— London, United Kingdom

In 1766, James Christie opened his London auction house and launched the world's first fine art auctioneers. Some 210 years later, Christie's South Kensington was launched. Christie's first sold teddy bears in the early 1970's, often with a simple description like "a teddy bear — 20in." During the early 1980's, as the interest in teddy bears grew, a record price was achieved for a teddy bear in every sale. Then, in 1989, an amazing price of £12,100 (approximately $19,580) was paid for *Alfonzo*, a rare red Steiff teddy bear.

Lelya Maniera took over the bear mantle in 1992 and introduced the first all-bear sale in December 1993. The star of this sale was *Elliot*, a blue Steiff bear who sold for £49, 500 (approximately $73,250). A year later, the star was *Teddy Girl* selling for a world-record price of £110,000 (approximately $171,600). This record still stands for an old teddy bear, although a modern bear had sold for more. Christie's continues to hold two sales a year in May and December each devoted to teddy bears and soft toys—the only major auction house to do so. All auction catalogs appear online at their website two weeks prior to the auction.

TOP: IN 1989, IAN POUT PURCHASED *ALFONZO* AT CHRISTIE'S AUCTION HOUSE IN LONDON. *ALFONZO* WAS NOT LARGE IN SIZE 13IN (33CM) BUT HIS CHARISMA WAS AWESOME. TO THE AMAZEMENT OF THOSE IN THE SALESROOM AT THE TIME, IAN PAID A SETTING RECORD PRICE OF £12,000 (APPROXIMATELY $19,580) FOR HIM. *ALFONZO* WAS ORIGINALLY GIVEN BY GRAND DUKE GEORGE MICHAILOVICH TO HIS DAUGHTER, PRINCESS XENIA, IN 1908. *COURTESY TEDDY BEARS OF WITNEY.*

BOTTOM: DANIEL AGNEW, CHRISTIE'S SOUTH KENSINGTON TEDDY BEAR EXPERT, IS IN CHARGE OF THE TEDDY BEAR SALES. DANIEL IS PICTURED WITH CHRISTIE'S DECEMBER 4, 2000 CHRISTIE'S AUCTION CATALOG AND THE EXTREMELY RARE 1912 STEIFF 19-½IN (50CM) BLACK BEAR THAT BROUGHT A REALIZED PRICE OF £91,750 (APPROXIMATELY $136,248) AT THE DECEMBER 2000 AUCTION.

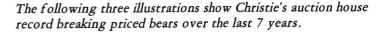

*The following three illustrations show Christie's auction house record breaking priced bears over the last 7 years.*

*ELLIOT.* STEIFF BEAR. 1908. 13IN (33CM) UNIQUE BLUE MOHAIR; SHOE-BUTTON EYES; FULLY-JOINTED; EXCELSIOR STUFFING. THE EXTENSIVE STEIFF COMPANY ARCHIVES REPORT THAT ONLY ONE BLUE STEIFF BEAR WAS CREATED; A HAND SAMPLE FOR THE DEPARTMENT STORE, HARRODS. *ELLIOT* WAS AMONG SIX VARIOUSLY COLORED TEDDY BEARS MADE BY STEIFF AND SENT TO HARRODS IN LONDON AS SAMPLE BEARS FOR FUTURE SPECIAL ORDERS. SADLY, *ELLIOT'S* UNIQUE COLOR DID NOT ATTRACT THE STORE'S BUYER AND THE CONTEMPORARY BLANK STEIFF ORDER FORM VERIFIES THAT HE WAS NEVER COMMERCIALLY MANUFACTURED. *ELLIOT* SOLD AT CHRISTIE'S SOUTH KENSINGTON DECEMBER 6, 1993 AUCTION FOR £49,500 (APPROXIMATELY $73,250). *COURTESY CHRISTIE'S.*

*TEDDY GIRL.* STEIFF BEAR. 1904. 18IN (46CM); CINNAMON MOHAIR; "CENTER SEAM" IN HEAD; SHOE-BUTTON EYES; FULLY-JOINTED; EXCELSIOR STUFFING. *TEDDY GIRL* WAS COL. HENDERSON'S LIFE-LONG COMPANION. FROM A VERY YOUNG AGE *TEDDY GIRL* AND COL. HENDERSON BECAME INSEPARABLE, TRAVELING EVERYWHERE TOGETHER. *TEDDY GIRL* NOT ONLY INSPIRED COL. HENDERSON TO DEVOTE A LARGE PART OF HIS LIFE TO GOOD BEARS OF THE WORLD BUT ALSO INSPIRED SO MANY OTHER DEVOTED TEDDY BEAR LOVERS TO COLLECT AND EVEN DESIGN THEIR OWN BEARS. *TEDDY GIRL* ALONG WITH MANY PHOTOGRAPHS OF COL. HENDERSON SOLD AT CHRISTIE'S SOUTH KENSINGTON DECEMBER 5, 1994 AUCTION FOR £110,000 (APPROXIMATELY $171,600). THE PROUD NEW OWNER, MR. YOSHIHIRO SEKIGUCHI SHOWCASES *TEDDY GIRL* IN HIS TEDDY BEAR MUSEUM IN IZU, JAPAN. *COURTESY CHRISTIE'S.*

*TEDDY EDWARD.* ENGLISH BEAR. CIRCA 1950. 13IN (33CM); GOLD MOHAIR; GLASS EYES; FULLY-JOINTED; EXCELSIOR STUFFING. THE NAME *TEDDY EDWARD* GOES BACK OVER 39 YEARS DURING WHICH TIME HE ESTABLISHED HIS REPUTATION AS ONE OF THE MOST TRAVELED TEDDY BEARS IN THE WORLD. HE HAS BEEN TO TIMBUCTU IN THE SAHARA DESERT, TO KHATMANDU *EN ROUTE* FOR EVEREST, AND TO THE BOTTOM OF THE GRAND CANYON AS WELL AS NEW YORK AND MANY EUROPEAN COUNTRIES INCLUDING THE GREEK ISLANDS. *TEDDY EDWARD* WAS SOLD AT CHRISTIE'S SOUTH KENSINGTON AUCTION ON DECEMBER 9, 1996 FOR £34,500 (APPROXIMATELY $50,690). *TEDDY EDWARD* WAS PURCHASED BY YOSHIHIRO SEKIGUCHI TO BE ONE OF THE STAR ATTRACTIONS FOR HIS TEDDY BEAR MUSEUM IN NASU, JAPAN. *COURTESY CHRISTIE'S.*

# The Bear Forest Internet Auction 2000 — Netherlands

In January 2000, Dutch teddy bear artist Judith Schnog conceived the idea for an Internet artist teddy bear auction to benefit the International Bear Foundation (IBF). Judith launched an appealed to renowned teddy bear artists around the world to create a bear and donate it to this worthy and wonderful organization. The response was overwhelming. By means of The Bear Forest Internet Auction 2000, IBF was able to inform the teddy bear world what was happening to brown bears in Europe and how IBF tries to help bears in distress. The entire funds raised from the auction will be spent on the care of the European brown bears in a unique sanctuary called *The Bear Forest* in Rhenen (Holland) and on IBF's dancing bear project in Bulgaria. The goal of the Bulgarian project is to have all of the dancing bears confiscated, which can only happen when a proper rescue center, like the Bear Forest, has been built. The auction raised $21,800 from the 55 artist bear donations.

**ABOVE:** BORA WAS ABUSED AS A DANCING BEAR IN THE TURKISH CITY OF ISTANBUL. HE WAS FOUND WANDERING ABOUT THE STREETS BLIND WITH AN INJURED NOSE. PLASTIC SURGERY HELPED PATCH UP HIS NOSE AND LIPS. BORA NOW LIVES SAFELY, HAPPILY, AND CONTENTEDLY IN THE BEAR FOREST IN RHENEN, HOLLAND. *COURTESY THE BEAR FOREST.*

**RIGHT:** GERMAN BEAR ARTIST ROTRAUD ILLISCH MADE *NELLY* FOR THE BEAR FOREST INTERNET AUCTION. *NELLY* IS ROTRAUD'S RENDITION OF THE REAL BEAR NELLY WHO, FOR MANY YEARS, EARNED A LIVING FOR GYPSIES WHO TRAVELED THROUGH YUGOSLAVIA. NELLY HAS SETTLED INTO HER NEW LIFE AT THE BEAR FOREST.

# *Teddy Bear Magazines*

There are a number of excellent magazines that focus on the teddy bear. These publications are a combination of art magazines, trade publications and references for collectors. Their audience is vast and includes collectors, artists, manufacturers, shopkeepers, suppliers and show promoters. Some of the best known are *Teddy Bear and Friends*, *Teddy Bear Times* and *Teddy Today*.

TOP: *TEDDY BEAR & FRIENDS'* MAGAZINE EDITOR, MINDY KINSEY, HOLDS A COPY OF THE MAGAZINE AND HER OWN CHILDHOOD BEAR, WHICH HER GRANDMOTHER MADE HER FOR CHRISTMAS. *TEDDY BEAR & FRIENDS* IS MANY THINGS—AN ART MAGAZINE, A TRADE PUBLICATION, AND A REFERENCE FOR COLLECTORS.

MIDDLE: *TEDDY BEAR TIMES* IS AN INFORMATIVE AND GLOSSY MONTHLY BRITISH MAGAZINE, WHICH CONSISTENTLY OFFERS ARTICLES BY LEADING FIGURES IN THE BEAR WORLD. *COURTESY TEDDY BEAR TIMES.*

BOTTOM: *TEDDY TODAY* IS THE BRAINCHILD OF DENIS SHAW (LEFT) AND JOHN PAUL PORT (RIGHT). BOTH ARE LONG-TIME TEDDY BEAR ARTISTS AND COLLECTORS WHO DECIDED TO THROW THEIR HATS INTO THE PUBLISHING WORLD IN THE SPRING OF 1997.

# Teddy Bear Associations

## Good Bears Of The World — Toledo, Ohio

The magic of the teddy bear is exemplified in The Good Bears of the World. The non-profit organization, founded in 1973 by James T. Ownby, provides teddy bears to sick children and hospitalized adults, elderly people confined to nursing homes, and abused children in shelters and foster homes. The goal of The Good Bears of the World (GBW) members (and their local "dens") is to make the teddy bear a symbol of hope and faith and through his powers, promote worldwide love, friendship and goodwill. In 1986, Jim Ownby passed away and the James T. Ownby Memorial Bear Bank was established as GBW's official vehicle for donating teddies. GBW has continued to grow and prosper thanks to the generosity, love and caring of the teddy bear industry. Each year, thousands of bears are donated to traumatized children and the elderly from the GBW Bear Bank and also by their local dens. GBW's quarterly publication, *Bear Tracks*, is distributed at shows from coast to coast and is sometimes an introduction to love and generosity of our industry to new collectors. The association also honors President Theodore Roosevelt on the anniversary of his birth with *Good Bear Day*, which is October 27.

For additional information on Good Bears of the World contact: Good Bears of the World, Box 13097, Toledo, OH 43613. Phone and Fax: (419) 531-5365. http://www.goodbearsoftheworld.org.

**ABOVE LEFT:** JIM OWNBY (LEFT) CONCEIVED THE GOOD BEARS OF THE WORLD IN 1969. THE CLUB WAS OFFICIALLY CHARTERED AND FOUNDED IN 1973. PETER BULL (RIGHT). *COURTESY GOOD BEARS OF THE WORLD.*

**ABOVE RIGHT:** THE JAMES T. OWNBY MEMORIAL BEAR BANK WAS CREATED TO MAKE SURE GOOD BEARS OF THE WORLD WILL ALWAYS BE ABLE TO SUPPLY THE TEDDY BEARS REQUESTED BY THOSE WHO MINISTER TO PEOPLE (PARTICULARLY CHILDREN AND THE ELDERLY) IN PAIN. *COURTESY GOOD BEARS OF THE WORLD.*

**RIGHT:** *BEAR TRACKS* IS PUBLISHED QUARTERLY BY GOOD BEARS OF THE WORLD. "PROJECT SMILES" WAS ONE OF THE NUMEROUS GOOD BEARS OF THE WORLD PROJECTS TO PROVIDE TEDDY BEARS TO HOSPITALIZED CHILDREN. *COURTESY GOOD BEARS OF THE WORLD.*

# The Japan Teddy Bear Association —
# Tokyo, Japan

The Japan Teddy Bear Association (JTBA) was established in 1993 as a voluntary group of teddy bear fans in Japan. Since then, the JTBA has been assisting the teddy bear artists in Japan. As of October 1999, the government recognized JTBA as a non-profit organization with a membership of 4,000 and 150 member shops and museums.

JTBA publishes a newsletter, *Teddy Bear Voice*, for their members 6 times a year. It covers various information about teddy bears not only in Japan, but also overseas. The *Teddy Bear Voice* offers assistance and advice to teddy bear artists as a newsletter of a non-profit organization. To spread the charm of teddy bears and also to find talented artists, the JTBA sponsors teddy bear contests twice a year. One takes place in person at their annual convention in the summer. The other is decided based upon photos.

**ABOVE:** KAZUNDO ONOZUKA, FOUNDER AND CHAIRPERSON OF THE JAPAN TEDDY BEAR ASSOCIATION.

**TOP RIGHT:** THE *TEDDY BEAR VOICE* IS PUBLISHED SIX TIMES A YEAR BY THE JAPAN TEDDY BEAR ASSOCIATION.

**MIDDLE RIGHT:** ENTHUSIASTIC TEDDY BEAR COLLECTORS AT THE OPENING OF JAPAN TEDDY BEAR ASSOCIATION'S ANNUAL CONVENTION IN TOKYO, JAPAN.

**BOTTOM RIGHT:** THE INCREASING CREATIVITY OF THE JAPANESE TEDDY BEAR ARTIST IS EXEMPLIFIED EACH YEAR IN THE COMPETITION ENTRIES AT THE JAPAN TEDDY BEAR ASSOCIATION'S CONVENTION.

*Chapter Five*

# The Magical Power of the Teddy Bear

*Every year, teddy's popularity and undeniable powers continue to grow. We all know that teddy bears have made the quality of life better for children throughout the years. As a symbol of love and caring, they offer security, comfort and companionship. The teddy bear's nurturing attributes are particularly important to unfortunate youngsters who have suffered mistreatment, parental desertion, and/or illness. Psychologists and psychiatrists say teddies represent security. Later in life, it is only natural that adults return to their trusted childhood pal, the teddy bear.*

Teddy bears promote comfort and safety, solace and companionship, warmth and love in numerous therapeutic instances. Teddy bears have helped premature infants overcome breathing problems. Teachers and speech therapists utilize teddy bears as vehicles to help children with speech and mental impairments as well as emotionally disturbed children to communicate. Police departments often use bears for children traumatized by abuse, injury, violence or death. I continue to witness the unbelievable magic of teddy's powers.

I'd like to inspire bear lovers to use our favorite toy to make life better for a child, the elderly or anyone that would benefit from having a teddy bear to hold. You may do this individually or through a group effort. For instance, my teddy bear show in San Diego raises funds to donate to worthwhile charities. So at each show, the other collectors/exhibitors and I personally donate bears from our own collection to raise funds for various charities. The response has been wonderful. I am proud to say our efforts have raised over $50,000 since my first event in 1983.

The following two stories are beautiful examples of love, strength and teddy bear power:

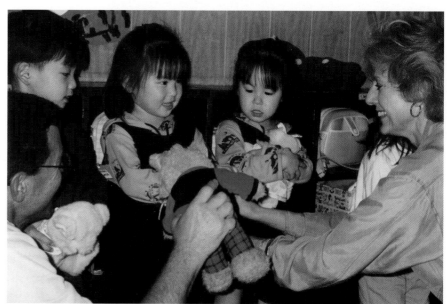

TOP: LINDA MULLINS WITNESSED THE MIRACLE OF THE TEDDY BEAR FIRST HAND WHEN SHE HELPED HAND-DELIVER OVER 2,000 TEDDY BEARS TO THE CHILDREN WHO WERE ORPHANED BY THE TERRIBLE KOBE EARTHQUAKE IN 1995. LINDA AND WALLY MULLINS AND RON AND ELKE BLOCK PUT TOGETHER TEDDY BEAR RELIEF INTERNATIONAL. TOGETHER THEY JOINED HANDS TO COMFORT THE VICTIMS OF THE TRAGEDY WITH TEDDY BEARS.

BOTTOM: MARCELLA JOHNSON (CENTER), FOUNDER OF THE COMFORT CUB, DELIVERS HER BEARS TO REPRESENTATIVES OF THE SAN DIEGO HOSPICE FOUNDATION AND SAN DIEGO HOSPICE CHILDREN'S PROGRAM.

# San Diego Hospice and the Comfort Cub Program

By Marcella Johnson

The loss of a baby is one of the most devastating experiences in the world — not only emotionally but physically as well. The Comfort Cub was created to help the healing process of a mother who has experienced the heart breaking death of her child.

My sweet little baby, George, was born on April 11, 1999 and died just 15 minutes later. Along with the obvious emotional pain I was feeling after baby George died, I also experienced some painful physical symptoms as well. It wasn't until a week or so later when I realized what the pain was. My arms longed to hold my new baby. When I held an object that was about the right size, weight and circumference of a new baby my aching went away. That's when I got the idea to create a *Comfort Cub*—a weighted teddy bear for a mother to hold when her arms hurt and her heart is aching. That was the beginning of the Comfort Cub Program. The bear is also distributed to all mothers who loose a baby at San Diego's Sharp Mary Birch Hospital and at Children's Hospital. Our hope is to expand our program to reach out to as many families who experience the loss of a baby that we can.

If you are interested in the Comfort Cub Program, you can contact the San Diego Hospice Foundation at 4311 Third Avenue, San Diego, CA 92103 (619) 688-1600.

# Sir Koff-A-Lot & Kiddie Kub

Doctors Lawrence and Carolyn Shaffer, two cardiovascular surgeons whose patients found post-operative respiratory therapy very painful, developed *Sir Koff-A-Lot* and the *Kiddie Kub* teddy bears. After a heart by-pass or abdominal or thoracic surgery, patients are required to "cough" in order to avoid respiratory complications. Holding firmly to a *Sir-Koff-A-Lot* makes the pain a little more bearable because it acts as a splint against the incision. But equally important, it gives patients, regardless of their age, something to hug.

Since their development in 1984, over 300,000 patients recovering from surgery have used the bears. The bears also provide psychotherapeutic benefits to patients by becoming their "friends" during recovery.

For additional information on *Sir-Koff-A-Lot* bears contact: Muffin Enterprises Inc. 1 Brenneman Circle, Suite 2, Mechanicsburg, PA 17055, USA. Tel: (800) 338-9041. (717) 691-9800. Fax: (717) 691-9803. E-mail: muffin@pa.net.

RECOVERING CARDIAC PATIENT USING *SIR-KOFF-A-LOT* DURING RESPIRATORY THERAPY.

## Chapter Six

# To Teddy With Love . . .

I am blessed because both my mother and father raised me with love. This unconditional love has transformed me into a caring human being with a deep passion for life. My beloved mother, who passed away in 1998, instilled in me a belief that with compassion, one can heal a wounded soul and that our children are the roots of kindness . . . so we have the responsibility to behold them ever so tenderly. Her wisdom helped me believe in spreading my wings, taking chances and finding the goodness in people. This is why revisiting my homeland, Vietnam is the calling of my life. To share my love and touch the hearts of our children, are the gifts that I can give to my mother for giving a voice in this world.

I also believe that with the love of a teddy bear, all things are possible! Dear Friends, spread your wings, take chances, find the goodness in people and follow your heart in the name of our beloved Teddy . . . with love.

Ho Phi Le 2001

OPPOSITE PAGE: MANY COLLECTORS OF ANTIQUE DOLLS ALSO COLLECT TEDDY BEARS. THIS EARLY 1900'S STEIFF BEAR IS IN THE ROYAL COMPANY OF A RARE GERMAN SIMON & HAILBIG #1488 ANTIQUE DOLL. *PHOTOGRAPH BY HO PHI LE.*

ABOVE: THE ENDEARING EXPRESSION ON THIS BEAUTIFUL GIRL'S FACE EXEMPLIFIES THE BOND BETWEEN A CHILD AND HER BELOVED COMPANION, TEDDY. *PHOTOGRAPH BY HO PHI LE.*

TOP RIGHT: COLLECTOR SUSAN WILEY'S PRETTY GRANDDAUGHTER, CHRISTINA OLSON, SHARES HER GRANDMOTHER'S LOVE OF TEDDY BEARS. *PHOTOGRAPH BY HO PHI LE.*

RIGHT: HO PHI LE AT 4 YEARS OLD WITH HIS BELOVED MOTHER.

AMY AFFECTIONATELY GAZES AT
HER EARLY 1900 CENTER SEAM
STEIFF BEAR. AMY IS WEARING AN
ANTIQUE COAT AND HAT MADE OF
THE SAME LUXURIOUS WHITE
MOHAIR AS HER BELOVED BEAR.
PHOTOGRAPH BY HO PHI LE.

**TOP:** YOUNG CHRISTOPHER SMITH SHARES SOME QUIET QUALITY TIME WITH HIS FRIEND AND CONFIDANTE TEDDY. *PHOTOGRAPH BY HO PHI LE.*

**BOTTOM:** WELL-KNOWN PHOTOGRAPHER HO PHI LE'S OUTSTANDING PHOTOGRAPHS OF CHILDREN WITH TEDDY BEARS HAVE DELIGHTED TEDDY BEAR LOVERS AROUND THE WORLD SINCE 1985. *PHOTOGRAPH BY HO PHI LE.*

*A Short Message to my Readers:*

*For the past century, our beloved Teddy Bear has loved and comforted people all over the world, and we have loved him back, unconditionally. In this spirit of love, I invite you all to support my life long goal. Please help me make the Teddy Bear an international ambassador of good will and, thorough his magical powers, bring people from every corner of the earth closer together.*

*Thank you,*
*Linda Mullins*

LINDA AND WALLY MULLINS WITH THEIR PET POODLE NIKKI AND ONE OF THEIR FAVORITE EARLY 1900'S STEIFF BEARS.

*About the Author*

Linda Mullins was born and raised in England. She immigrated to America in 1969. Her present collection of more than 2,000 bears began in earnest when her husband, Wally, gave her an antique teddy bear as a gift. That hobby escalated to a full-time profession, and today, Linda Mullins' knowledge and expertise are in demand throughout the United States, Europe and the Pacific Rim.

A Southern California resident, she produces the region's most popular two-day show: *Linda's San Diego Teddy Bear, Doll & Antique Toy Show and Sale.* It is held twice a year. The January show of 2001 was the 46th of these events. They continue to draw international attention because of the excellent antique, collectible and artist Teddy Bears, Dolls and Toys on exhibit and available for purchase. In addition to collecting, speaking, educating and traveling, Linda has written 18 books and countless articles on the past, present and future of teddy bears.

She and her husband Wally are currently building a new residence for themselves and their bears in their hometown of Carlsbad, California. The Victorian-style manor will incorporate a private museum to house Linda's extensive bear and toy collection along with Wally's sizeable assembly of music box and band organs.

After an all-out effort coordinating an auction of international artist's bears designed to raise funds for Kobe, Japan's earthquake victims, Linda Mullins became instrumental in shaping that country's Huis Ten Bosch's Teddy Bear Kingdom in Nagasaki, Japan. She is honored to be a supervisor and honorary director of the museum. It is Linda's lifelong goal to continue on her mission to make the teddy bear an ambassador of world love and peace.